Philosophy of the Earlier Stoics

The Rediscovered Philosophers
Books in this Series

The series is edited by Charles Siegel.

Philosophy of the Earlier Stoics

works by

Diogenes of Babylon, Panaetius, Posidonius, Cicero and Others

edited with introductions
by Charles Siegel

Omo Press

adolescentium alunt
senectutem oblectant

ISBN 978-1-941667-09-5

Cover picture: Raphael, The School of Athens (1509-1511)

Contents

Note: Cicero wrote an exposition of the Stoics' view of determinism and free will in his book *De Fato* (*On Fate*), but it is lost. The book of *De Fato* that survives, where Cicero criticizes the Stoics from the viewpoint of the skeptical Academy, has a great deal of information about the Stoic view of determinism and is included in *Philosophy of the Skeptical Academy*.

Translations

The Rediscovered Philosophers series uses the following translations of Cicero's works, which are all in the public domain. Translations have been modified to bring them into conformity with contemporary American spelling conventions and to create consistent spelling of philosophers' names and consistent transliterations of Greek words.

Subheadings have been added and text has sometimes been broken into smaller paragraphs for readability.

Quotations from these works always refer to these translations and footnotes to these editions.

Academica (Academic Questions)

M. T. Cicero, *The Academic Questions*, *Treatise De Finibus*. and *Tusculan Disputations*, Literally translated by C. D. Yonge, B.A. (London: George Bell and Sons, 1875).

De Divinatione (On Divination)

M.T. Cicero, *On the nature of the gods*, *On divination*, *On fate*, *On the republic*, *On the laws*, and *On standing for the consulship*. Literally translated chiefly by C.D. Yonge, B.A (London: George Bell and Sons, 1878).

De Fato (On Fate)

Cicero, *De Senectute*, *De Amicitia*, and *De Fato*, translated by W. A. Falconer (Loeb Classical Library, Harvard University Press, 1923).

De Finibus Bonorum et Malorum (On the Ends of Good and Evil)

Cicero, *De Finibus*, translated by H. Harris Rackham. (Loeb Classical Library, Harvard University Press, vol. XVII, second (revised) edition, 1931).

De Legibus (The Laws)

The Political Works of Marcus Tullius Cicero: Treatise on the Commonwealth and Treatise on the Laws, translated by Francis Barham (London, Edmund Spettigue, 1842).

De Natura Deorum (On the Nature of the Gods)

Cicero, *De Natura Deorum* and *Academica*, translated by H. Harris Rackham. (Loeb Classical Library, Harvard University Press, 1933.)

De Officiis (On Duties)

Marcus Tullius Cicero, *De Officiis*, translated by Walter Miller (Cambridge, Harvard University Press, Loeb Classical Library, 1913).

De Republica (On the Republic or On the Commonwealth)

Cicero's *Tusculan Disputations*; Also, Treatises *On The Nature Of The Gods*, And *On The Commonwealth*. Literally translated chiefly by C. D. Yonge. (New York: Harper & Brothers, 1877).

Tusculanae Quaestiones (Tusculan Disputations)

Cicero's Tusculan Disputations; Also, Treatises On The Nature Of The Gods, And On The Commonwealth. Literally translated chiefly by C. D. Yonge. (New York: Harper & Brothers, 1877).

About the Authors

Diogenes of Babylon

Diogenes of Babylon (230 to 220 - 150 to140 BC) was born in Seleucia, a city on the Tigris River in Babylon. Seleucia was one of the three great Hellenistic capital cities left after Alexander's empire dissolved, less important as a center of culture than Alexandria (in Egypt) and more important than Antioch (in Syria).

He studied in Athens under Chrysippus, the most systematic of the Stoic philosophers, and he became scholarch of the Stoic school in Athens in the second century BC. He seems to have followed the thinking of Chrysippus.

He was one of the three philosophers who were sent to Rome in 155 BC to convince the Romans to revoke a fine of 500 Talents that they had imposed on Athens as a punishment for their destruction of the town of Oropus. He lectured in Rome and was admired by the Romans for his temperate and sober way of speaking[1] — unlike the Academic philosopher Carneades who accompanied him and whose second lecture on Justice (included in Philosophy of the Skeptical Academy) scandalized the Romans by arguing for moral relativism.

Cicero called him "a great and highly esteemed Stoic."[2]

Panaetius

Panaetius of Rhodes (c. 185 - c. 110/09 BC) was a student at the Stoic school in Athens of Diogenes of Babylon and of Antipater of Tarsus, Diogenes' successor as scholarch.

He moved to Rome where he was associated with the

---

1 Aulus Gellius, *Attic Nights* VII: 14, Cicero, *Academica* II: xlv.
2 *De Officiis* III: xii.

group of intellectuals who gathered around Scipio Africanus the younger, helping to introduce Stoic ideas to Rome. When Scipio died in 129 BC, he moved back to Athens, and he succeeded Antipater of Tarsus (who died at about the same time) as scholarch of the Stoic school.

He rejected some doctrines of earlier Stoics and was more willing to accept the doctrines of other schools, and so he is considered the founder of the second Stoa. For example, he denied the old Stoic belief that periodic conflagrations destroyed the world and instead accepted Aristotle's belief that that the world endures forever. He also was the only major Stoic thinker who did not believe in divination.

Unlike earlier Stoics, he believed that people could move gradually toward virtue. His work *On Duties*, the basis of Cicero's *On Duties*, was considered a turning point in Stoic thought, because it gave advice that ordinary people could apply in their everyday life, while earlier Stoics gave advice that applied to the ideal wise man.

Posidonius

Posidonius (c. 135 BCE – c. 51 BCE) was admired for his contributions to many fields of knowledge, including astronomy, physics, mathematics, geography and history, as well as philosophy.

To give some examples, he wrote a continuation of the *World History* of Polybius; he wrote ethnographic studies of the Celts of Gaul; he calculated the circumference of the earth by comparing the angle of the star Canopus above the horizon at Rhodes and Alexandria, correcting for the refraction of light passing through the earth's atmosphere; he constructed an orrery, a mechanical model of heavenly bodies revolving around the earth, which was so large that it was powered by walking on a treadmill.

He was a student of Panaetius, and he also was willing to accept opinions of other schools of philosophy and fuse them with Stoic thought, but he did not stray as far from traditional Stoic thought as Panaetius did.

A story that Cicero repeats shows that Posidonius lived up to his Stoic philosophy. When Pompey went to visit him, Posidonius was seriously ill with an attack of gout. Pompey went to Posidonius' bedside to tell him that he was sorry that he was not well enough to discourse on philosophy, but Posidonius insisted on delivering a discourse on the Stoics' belief that nothing is good except what is morally honorable—and whenever he had a sudden paroxysm of pain, he said "Pain, it is to no purpose; … I will never acknowledge you an evil."[3]

Cicero

Marcus Tullius Cicero was one of the greatest Roman statesmen and orators. He was born on January 3, 106 BC to a wealthy family of the equestrian class, the class immediately below the patricians.

As a youth, Cicero studied philosophy with Phaedrus the Epicurean, Diodotus the Stoic, and Philo the Academic, who all came to Rome to escape the Mithridatic War in Athens. In 79-77 BC, he went to Athens to study with Phaedrus and Zeno the Epicureans and with Antiochus the Academic, and then to Rhodes, where he became friends with Posidonius the Stoic. In 51 BC, he visited Aristus (Antiochus' brother and successor) in Athens and Cratippus the Peripatetic in Mytilene. Diodotus the Stoic lived in Cicero's house in Rome for many years, continuing to teach him philosophy and logic until he died in 59 BC, when Cicero was in his late forties.

In Rome, he followed the standard path of political advancement, becoming a quaestor in 75 BC, aedile in 69 BC, and praetor in 66 BC. In 63 BC, he was elected one of the two consuls, Rome's highest political office. He was elected to these offices at the minimum allowable age.

---

3 *Tusculanae Quaestiones* II: xxvi.

As consul, he defeated Catiline's conspiracy to overthrow the republic, and the Senate proclaimed him "Savior of the Republic" and "Father of his Fatherland." During the power struggle between Caesar and Pompey, he supported Pompey because he considered him more likely to preserve the republic. After Caesar became dictator, Cicero withdrew from government and spent his time writing, translating the ideas of Greek philosophers into Latin and inventing much of the philosophical vocabulary that we have used ever since.

Cicero revealed his own attitude toward this work when he wrote:

> "now, having been stricken to the ground by a most severe blow of fortune, and being discharged from all concern in the republic, I seek a medicine for my sorrow in philosophy, and consider this study the most honorable pastime for my leisure ... inferior to no other occupation in its usefulness for the purpose of educating my fellow-countrymen. Or even if this be too high a view to take of it, at all events I see nothing else which I can do."[4]

After Caesar's death, Cicero returned to politics, opposing Mark Antony in a series of speeches that were named the Philippics after Demosthenes' speeches opposing Phillip of Macedon. Antony, Lepidus, and Octavian (who later became the emperor Augustus) gained power as the second triumvirate on November 27, 43 BC, when the *Lex Titia* was passed, giving them the power to make and annul laws without consent of the senate or the people and to make judicial decisions that could not be appealed. Though Octavian argued against it, the triumvirate added Cicero to its list of enemies of the state. On December 7, 43 BC, Cicero was caught and murdered as he tried to reach a ship and flee to Macedonia. On Antony's instructions, his head and hands were cut off and displayed in the forum.

4 *Academica* I: iii.

Introduction to the Series
by Charles Siegel

This series of books makes it possible to read classical philosophers whose works have been inaccessible since ancient times.

When you start to study classical philosophy, you read Plato and Aristotle, and you learn that four schools dominated philosophy after their time, during the Hellenistic and Roman periods.

The Epicureans believed that the universe was infinite and was made up of atoms that combined by chance. The good life was devoted to pleasure, which consists primarily of absence of pain in the body and of disquiet in the soul.

The Stoics believed that the universe as a whole had a mind and shaped events providentially. The good life was devoted to virtue, and the wise and virtuous man was perfectly happy regardless of misfortune or pain.

The Peripatetics continued the work of Aristotle, but they became less important during Hellenistic times.

The Academics continued the work of Plato, but the Academy changed dramatically during its history. A century after Plato, it became skeptical and denied that there was any knowledge. Centuries later, the Academic Antiochus of Ascalon began to claim that the Peripatetics, the Stoics, and the old Academy of Plato all had the same beliefs, and he synthesized the ideas of these schools.

But after you have read the basic descriptions of these later classical schools, if you want to go further and read their philosophy, you soon become frustrated. Some writing of the Epicureans survives, including short works by Epicurus himself and a long book by Lucretius. Very little philosophy of the Stoics survives: there are books by late

Stoics with advice about how to live a good life, but little or nothing with their philosophical theories. No complete works of the Peripatetics or later Academics survive, just fragments.

The only consecutive exposition of these philosophies is in Cicero's dialogs, where prominent Romans argue for and against Stoicism, the skeptical Academy, and the syncretic Academy, but these dialogs are hard to read because they contain extraneous material and are sometimes disorganized.

Typically, you learn about these later classical philosophers by reading descriptions of their philosophies based on fragments and testimonies. Imagine learning about Plato or William James by reading descriptions of their beliefs! You would not see how they defended their beliefs and you would miss out entirely on their personalities.

Cicero's Dialogs

Yet the works of these later classical philosophers are actually available, hidden in plain sight within Cicero's dialogs. Cicero wrote his most important works on philosophy and rhetoric in just two years, 46 BC to 44 BC, and he was capable of such large output because he took much of the text from other sources. Cicero himself admits in a letter to Atticus that his dialogs include his translations of earlier philosophical works:

> You will say — "What, when you write on such subjects [philosophy]?" They are translations. They don't cost so much trouble therefore; I only contribute the language, in which I am well provided.[5]

Cicero wrote elsewhere that he translated but also did more:

> ...for our part we do not fill the office of a mere translator, but, while preserving the doctrines

5 Cicero, *Epistulae ad Atticum* CXCVII translated in Evelyn Shuckburgh, *The Letters of Cicero* (London, 1899-1900).

> of our chosen authorities, add thereto our own
> criticism and our own arrangement....[6]

And Cicero's works themselves make it clear that he also
made the Greek philosophical works more appealing to
Roman gentlemen by framing them as dialogs, where
the words of the philosophers were put in the mouths of
prominent Romans, adding lengthy accounts of the speakers'
gentlemanly behavior. He also added many illustrations of
his points from Roman history and many quotations from
literature; to give just one example, his book on divination
includes a very long poem that he wrote about his own term
as consul and about the portents that occurred then.[7]

These additions made the books more popular at the
time, and Cicero (as a character in one dialog) tells another
character how much he enjoyed them:

> Quintus, you have defended the Stoic doctrine
> with accuracy and like a Stoic. But the thing that
> delights me most is the fact that you illustrated
> your argument with many incidents taken from
> Roman sources—incidents, too, of a distinguished
> and noble type.[8]

But for today's student of philosophy, these additions are
obstacles in the way of the philosophical writing that is our
real interest.

Even more confusing, Cicero sometimes has speakers
deliver long discourses that combine incompatible material
from several sources.

Sometimes the material included in a single discourse
is repetitive, making it difficult to read. For example, his
defense of Stoic theology in *De Natura Deorum* Book II,
follows the Stoics' usual fourfold division of the subject,
discussing the existence of the gods, the nature of the gods,
the gods' government of the world, and the gods' care for
man. But Cicero took this material from four different Stoic

6 *De Finibus* I: ii.
7 *De Divinatione* I: x-xiii.
8 *De Divinatione* II: iii.

works, one on each of the four divisions, and he did not edit them for consistency. The first section is an exhaustive collection of Stoic arguments for the existence of the gods, but it also talks incidentally about the nature of the gods, which should be in the second section. The third section begins by discussing the existence of the gods, repeating ideas that were developed at length in the first section. The individual source works that he uses are generally well organized in themselves, but they are combined to form discourses that can be repetitive and badly organized.

Sometimes added material is out of place. For example, in the first half of *Academica* Book I, the speaker gives us an overview of the philosophy of Antiochus of Ascalon, founder of the Syncretic Academy, dividing philosophy into ethics, natural philosophy, and logic. Then, the same speaker adds a summary of Stoic philosophy that uses the same division into ethics, natural philosophy, and logic. Because this speaker is supposedly defending the ideas of Antiochus, we get the impression on first reading that this added section represents Antiochus' summary of the Stoics' ideas, but this is impossible: a central point of Antiochus' philosophy is that Stoics have the same ideas as Peripatetics and Academics and only use different language to state these ideas, and this concluding section is all about the substantive differences of the Stoics from these other schools. At the end, Cicero (as a character in the dialog) corrects the error of Cicero (as an editor) by saying that this does not really reflect Antiochus' view of the Stoics.

Cicero admitted in one of his dialogs that his writing is sometimes not unified, saying he could not write history because he did not have the leisure to produce cohesive works:

> Why certain spare times occur to every man, and
> these I was unwilling to lose. For instance, if I
> spent a few days in rusticating at my country seat,
> I employed them in composing a part of the essays
> I had determined to write. But for an historical
> work, it is impossible to do it justice unless one

can procure a regular vacation for a considerable period. My mind is thrown into a miserable state of suspense, when after fairly commencing a literary task, I am obliged to defer its conclusion to a future occasion; nor can I so easily recover the train of ideas in works so interrupted, as bring my essays to their appropriate conclusion, without rest or intermission.[9]

When you break up Cicero's dialogs into their source works, it becomes very clear that he sometimes combined disparate sources in disorganized ways.

Revealing the Source Works

This series of books, The Rediscovered Philosophers, edits Cicero's dialogs to reveal the source documents behind them. It removes most of the descriptions of gentlemanly activities, of the examples from Roman history and of the quotations from literature, so you can read the philosophy without this extraneous matter. It breaks up the dialogs, presenting each source document as a separate work and identifying the author when possible. It arranges these works by school, so you can study each philosophy without interruption.

In some cases, Cicero gives us hints that let us identify the authors of these source works. In other cases, we can guess at the author. And in other cases, we can only say that a work is by an unidentified source from one of the schools—but I hope that this series of books will lead to research that could identify some more of these sources.

This series of books keeps a bit of the framing that Cicero added to incorporate these sources in dialogs, because it is not possible to reconstruct the original texts precisely. Sometimes Cicero interjects comments by the speakers and modifies the original text to accommodate the interjections. Sometimes he inserts the names of the dialogs' speakers where the original might have said "the Stoics believe"

9 *De Legibus* I: ii.

or "Posidonius believes." We would have to alter these changes in arbitrary ways to make the works read like the source documents. By retaining the dialog form, we avoid these arbitrary decisions but still let the reader get a very clear look at the source works.

Even more important, retaining the dialog form lets readers see how the source works fit into Cicero's dialogs, so they can decide for themselves whether we have identified them correctly. In cases where one discourse contains multiple source documents, we keep the source documents in the same order that they have in the dialog, and we retain the dialog framing, so readers can see the inconsistencies in the whole discourse that show it was patched together from multiple source documents.

Some discourses are unified wholes, based on a single source work. Other discourses have repetitions and stylistic inconsistencies but can be broken into individual source works that are unified wholes.

When we see how some discourses are patched together, it becomes clear that Cicero simply translated source works, with minor changes, rather than writing the dialogs himself to illustrate the ideas of different schools of philosophy. There are cases where he did the writing himself or did extensive rewriting and produced more unified discourses, but they are less common.

This series of books keeps Cicero's brief comments on his translations of Greek philosophical terms into Latin, because they are of historical interest. It also adds subheadings and sometimes breaks up the works into smaller paragraphs to make the works more readable.

Benefits of this Series

These books make it easy, for the first time, to read works by the Stoics Chrysippus, Posidonius, Panaetius, and Diogenes of Babylon, by the skeptical Academics Carneades, Clitomachus, and Philo of Larissa, by the syncretic Academic Antiochus of Ascalon, and by unidentified authors from these schools.

Scholars have argued extensively about the sources of Cicero's dialogs. This series does not review all of the opinions of scholars about sources, but it can help to clarify the issues by revealing the original source works. For example, scholars have debated about the source of the discourse by Cicero (as a character in the dialog) criticizing Antiochus in the second half of *Academica* Book II,[10] but when you prepare an edition that breaks the dialogs up into individual source works, it becomes very obvious that Cicero's discourse is based on four different source works, differing noticeably in style, which have been published as "Four Works Defending Skepticism" in *Philosophy of the New Academy*. Though scholars have tried, it is obviously impossible to identify a single author of an inconsistent discourse written by multiple authors.

We hope that scholars will make more progress in identifying the sources by looking at the source works separately.

Most scholars give equal value to everything in Cicero's dialogs. It should also advance scholarship when they realize that these dialogs include multiple sources of widely varying quality.

Finally, we hope the public will become better acquainted with philosophical gems that are now almost unknown. Carneades' "Second Lecture on Justice" is one of the most notorious works of classical philosophy: the establishment was so shocked by its moral relativism that it rushed Carneades out of Rome; it is included in *Philosophy of the Skeptical Academy*. Antiochus of Ascalon's essay, which we have named "On Ethics," is the best surviving statement of classical virtue ethics, clearer and more to the point than

---

10 For example, see John Glucker, *Antiochus and the Late Academy*, (Gottingen, Vandenhoeck & Ruprecht, *Hypomnemata: Untersuchungen zur Antike und zu Ihrem Nachleben*, heft 56, p. 412 et seq. Glucker says that the source of this speech cannot be a work of Clitomachus, because it criticizes Antiochus, who was born after Clitomachus died. But it becomes easy to identify Clitomachus' contribution when we break it into its four source works; in fact, Cicero says explicitly that Clitomachus is the source of two of these works.

anything that survives from Aristotle or Thomas Aquinas. These works have been buried in Cicero's dialogs and known to only a handful of classical scholars, but now they are accessible to a wider audience.

Introduction to this Book
by Charles Siegel

The philosophy of Stoicism was intended to provide peace of mind, like the philosophy of Epicureanism, which became popular at about the same time — though the Stoics' advice was very different from the Epicureans'.

Many of its doctrines seem strange unless we remember their purpose. Philosophy was considered a guide to living a good life, and many young people flocked to the schools of philosophy to learn the wisdom to live well. We tend to forget this now that philosophy has become primarily an intellectual pursuit for academic specialists.

Ethics

The three branches of classical philosophy were ethics, natural philosophy (which included theology) and logic (which included epistemology). Of the three, ethics was the most important to the Stoics.

Stoic ethics begins with the idea that, by nature, all living things seek to survive and thrive. Plants seek the sunlight. Animals seek the food that nourishes them. People seek to thrive as animals do but also seek to thrive by gaining wealth, knowledge, health, physical strength, skill, and other natural advantages.

The virtues help us and others to gain these natural advantages, as we can see by looking at the four cardinal virtues, temperance, fortitude, prudence, and justice. Temperance helps us to protect our health. Fortitude and prudence help us to succeed at any endeavor. Justice implies that we should not pursue natural advantages for ourselves by sacrificing others: for example, we should not pursue wealth by stealing from or cheating others. Today, we generally think of ethics as a matter of acting altruistically or of treating others fairly, but to understand classical ethics, we must remember that the virtues were also means of living a successful and happy life.

The Stoics added this twist to virtue ethics: they said that only the virtues themselves were good. The natural advantages that the virtues aimed at were not good. They were indifferent, but they were "preferred" or "to be chosen" or "valuable."

Cicero sums up this idea very well in a passage based on the writing of the Stoic philosopher Diogenes of Babylon:

> ...this which we entitle preferred or superior is neither good nor evil; and accordingly we define it as being indifferent but possessed of a moderate value .... For in fact, it was inevitable that the class of intermediate things should contain some things that were either in accordance with nature, or the reverse, and this being so, that this class should include some things which possessed moderate value, and, granting this, that some things of this class should be 'preferred.'[11]

Sometimes the Stoics described these natural advantages as "preferred indifferents," which seems like a self-contradiction.

In fact, the theory is problematic: if the natural advantages are "valuable" and "to be chosen," then why not call them good? Diogenes of Babylon tried to explain it by saying:

> It will be an error to infer that this view implies two Ultimate Goods. For though if a man were to make it his purpose to take a true aim with a spear or arrow at some mark, his ultimate end, corresponding to the ultimate good as we pronounce it, would be to do all he could to aim straight: the man in this illustration would have

11 *De Finibus*, III: xvi, included in this book as part of the work "On the System of Stoic Ethics" by or after Diogenes of Babylon.

> to do everything to aim straight, yet, although he
> did everything to attain his purpose, his 'ultimate
> End,' so to speak, would be what corresponded to
> what we call the Chief Good in the conduct of life,
> whereas the actual hitting of the mark would be in
> our phrase 'to be chosen' but not 'to be desired.'[12]

In other words, if you are practicing archery, your real goal is to be as skillful as possible at archery; hitting the target is not important in itself but is chosen to exercise your skill.

The flaw in this argument is that archery practice is a game with an arbitrary goal that you play to improve your skill. It is very different to seek some natural advantage. If a doctor tries his best to cure a patient but the patient dies anyway, would we say that it is not important whether the patient dies, because the doctor's goal is to behave virtuously? If a man tries his best to feed his family, would we say that it is not important whether the family starves, because the man's goal is to behave virtuously? These goals are natural advantages, given by nature, rather than being arbitrary.

If the virtues are aimed at gaining natural advantages, why should we say that the virtues are good but the goals they aim at are not good?

The Stoics made this distinction in order to put your happiness completely under your own control. A wise man is virtuous. Virtue is the only good and so is the only thing needed for happiness. Therefore, a wise man will be perfectly happy because of his virtue, regardless of his external conditions. Even if he is being tortured or even if he is starving to death, he will not lack any good thing and so will be perfectly happy.

It is logically problematic to say that the virtues are aimed at the goal of gaining practical advantages and that it does not matter whether they actually reach this goal, but it was psychologically helpful to the Stoics, helping them to achieve peace of mind.

---

12 Cicero, *De Finibus*, III: xvi.

Natural Philosophy and Theology

Natural philosophy (what we would now call attempts at science) and theology were considered a single subject in the three-fold Hellenistic division of philosophy. We should be able to see the connection by considering how scientific discoveries such as the theory of evolution have affected religious belief in our own time.

Stoicism also combined natural philosophy and theology in its key idea that all of nature has a mind, which governs the world for the benefit of all living things.[13] Mind is made up of a fiery substance in early Stoicism and of a mixture of fire and air among later Stoics. This substance pervades the entire universe and gives it mind, just as it pervades our bodies and gives us mind.

The mind of the universe is god, and its benevolent government of the universe is providence. Whenever there is suffering or imperfection in the universe, it is because providence directs the universe for the benefit of the whole and sometimes must sacrifice a part for the sake of the whole. The Stoics also believed that the stars were guided by intelligences and were gods, and that the traditional Greek and Roman gods were allegories representing abstractions or forces of nature.

This view of nature is deterministic. Providence governs the universe through a chain of causes and effects, with the causes inevitably producing the effects. The Stoics (with the exception of Panaetius) also believed in divination: as part of its care for us, providence gives us messages about the future, for example, in dreams. Divination requires determinism, since providence can tell us which future events will happen only if those events are bound to happen.

People have two choices. The wise man accepts everything that will happen to him as part of the providential government of the universe, realizing that even things that

13 This view was not invented by the Stoics. Xenophon attributes the same idea of god to Socrates in *Memorabilia* IV: 17 and the same idea of providence throughout *Memorabilia* IV, showing these ideas were current in Xenophon's time, a century before Zeno of Citium founded Stoicism.

cause him pain are necessary for the good of the universe as a whole, and so he has peace of mind. The foolish man tries to resist providence, fails, and so he can never have peace of mind. As the Stoics said, "Man is like a dog tied to a cart; if he does not walk along, he will pulled along."[14] We are not in control of events, but we are in control of our attitude toward events, and we can make ourselves happy by accepting providence rather than resisting it and being pulled along against our wills.

Like the Stoic view of virtue, this theory is meant to give us peace of mind and is logically problematic.

If we can choose our attitude, deciding either to "walk along" or "be pulled along," then we have some freedom of choice. But if our minds are fiery matter, and if the behavior of matter is determined by inevitable chains of cause and effect, then our attitude is determined, like everything else.

Different Stoic philosophers dealt with this contradiction in different ways.

Chrysippus said that our behavior is determined both by external events, which are their proximate cause, and by our character, which is their basic cause. By analogy, if someone pushes a cylinder and it rolls down hill, its motion has two causes: the proximate cause is someone pushing it, but the primary cause of its rolling is its own form as a cylinder. He said that our freedom is limited only if we are compelled to act by external causes, but the primary cause of a wise man's action is his own character.[15]

Chrysippus' claim that only one of the two causes matters is not convincing. The cylinder rolls both because of its shape and because it is pushed, and there is no good reason to say that the pushing is unimportant.

More fundamentally, Chrysippus just pushes the question back a step by claiming that that we are free if our actions are determined by our character. We still have to ask

14 A saying of Zeno and Chrysippus, cited and translated by J.M. Rist, Stoic Philosophy (Cambridge, Cambridge University Press, 1969) p. 127.

15 *De Fato*, xix. This description of Chrysippus' belief comes from discourse of a skeptical Academic, and so it is included in *Philosophy of the Skeptical Academy*, in a work titled "On Determinism and Freedom."

how we got our character. The cylinder got its shape because someone designed and produced it: it is problematic to say that its behavior is determined by its own shape and not by external causes, because its shape itself was determined by external causes. Likewise, it would be problematic to say that the wise man's behavior is not determined by external causes but by his character, if his character has been molded by external causes rather than his own free choices.

By contrast, the Stoic philosopher Cleanthes seems to reject the idea that providence determines all events that occur. In his *Hymn to Zeus*, where he praises Zeus as an allegorical representation of providence, he wrote:

> No work is wrought apart from Thee, O God,
> Or in the world, or in the heaven above,
> Or on the deep, save only what is done
> By sinners in their folly.
> …
> Thou hast fitted things
> Together, good and evil, that there reigns
> One everlasting Reason in them all.[16]

Here, Cleanthes preserves our freedom by saying that providence controls everything except moral choice: you are a sinner because you made this choice yourself, not because providence made you a sinner. Cleanthes' poem is reminiscent of the Christian view, where God gives us free will rather than determining our actions but governs the world so that even evil choices ultimately produce good. But the Stoics did not believe in an afterlife, so they did not have the Christians' consolation that the good will be rewarded and the wicked punished after death.

If we accept Cleanthes' idea of free will, we lose the Stoic consolation that all the evils that we face are caused by a wise providence because they are necessary to benefit the whole. If I am being tortured, my suffering is caused by the wickedness of the torturer. Even though providence

16 Cleanthes, the Stoic and Edward Henry Blakeney, *The Hymn of Cleanthes; Greek Text Translated. into English* (London, Society for Promoting Christian Knowledge; New York, Macmillan Co., 1921).

will ultimately direct it to good ends, my suffering is not caused by providence; and my suffering is not necessary for the good of the universe as a whole, since the universe as a whole would be even better if the person torturing me were wise rather than evil.

Despite its logical difficulties, this doctrine seems to have been psychologically useful to the Stoics. They accepted the hardships they faced, which they believed were caused by a wise providence. They also exercised their free will in constant efforts to be virtuous. Their determinism gave them the strength to face hardships, and their belief in their own free will let them make the effort to improve themselves, regardless of the contradiction between the two.

Epistemology

The Stoics needed an epistemology that let them claim they had certain knowledge, but the exact form of the Stoics' epistemology was not essential to their goal of gaining peace of mind.

Stoic epistemology is based on the idea that some perceptions are evidently true, which they called *phantasia katalêptikê*. *Phantasia* means "perception" or "sense impression." *Katalêpsis* means "comprehension." *Phantasia katalêptikê* can be translated as "comprehensible impression" and has also been translated as "recognizable impression"[17] or "cognitive impression."[18] Because it is a technical term and translations differ, many scholars adapt the Greek term and say "cataleptic perception" or "cataleptic impression."

The Stoics believed that all of our ideas were based on sense impression. When we are born, our minds are a blank slate (as Locke said). We form ideas by comparing multiple sense impressions. These ideas may be true or false, because our sense impressions may be true or false. For example, dreams and hallucinations are false.

---

17 Rist, *Stoic Philosophy,* p. 136.

18 A.A. Long, *Hellenistic Philosophy: Stoics, Epicureans, Sceptics,* second edition (Berkeley, University of California Press, 1986) p. 127.

But cataleptic impressions are true. They are defined as impressions that are caused by an outside object, are represented in our minds in a way that conforms to this object, and cannot come from anything else except this object.[19] Cicero tells us that Zeno, the founder of Stoicism, defined a cataleptic impression by saying "That it was such as is impressed and stamped upon and figured in us, according to and conformably to something which exists."[20]

The Academic skeptics argued that there was no such thing as a cataleptic perception. For example, if you see two identical objects, you get the same sense impression from them both, contrary to the Stoics' belief that a cataleptic impression conforms to an existing object and cannot come from anything else but that object. Nothing in your sense impressions tells you that they come from two different objects with identical appearance rather than from one object. To defend themselves against this argument, the Stoics were reduced to claiming that no two objects in the world were identical—hard for us to believe in our age of mass production.

This epistemology seems naive to us today. In the seventeenth century, as modern physics learned more about the nature of matter, philosophers realized that the ideas in our minds are qualitatively different from the physical objects that cause these ideas. For example, our perception of redness is qualitatively different from electromagnetic radiation with a wavelength of 650 nm, which causes this perception. This difference has been a central theme of philosophy since the time of Locke, Berkeley, and Hume, but most Hellenistic philosophy misses this issue completely. Aristotle dealt with it;[21] it seems plausible that his Peripatetic followers also dealt with it, though not enough of their work remains for us to know; but mainstream Hellenistic philosophy ignored it.

---

19 Rist, *Stoic Philosophy*, p. 137, citing Sextus Empiricus, Diogenes Laertius, and Cicero.

20   *Academica*, II: xxiv.

21   Aristotle, *Metaphysics*, IV: v.

Stoic epistemology was important historically, because it seems to have been the main or only epistemology used in Hellenistic times to claim that we can have knowledge. It was the epistemology that the Stoics developed to defend their beliefs, that the skeptics attacked to show we could have no knowledge, and that Antiochus of Ascalon adopted to defend his synthesis of Stoic, Peripatetic, and old Academic philosophy.

Stoicism as Wisdom Tradition

Though its philosophical ideas were problematic, Stoicism was a successful wisdom tradition. The idea that the virtues aim at natural advantages but that it makes absolutely no difference whether you get these natural advantages is problematic, but it apparently did help people to bear up under disappointments and failures. The idea that the universe is deterministic but that we should freely choose to follow the dictates of providence is problematic, but it apparently did help people to accept their lots in life.

Stoicism lasted longer as a wisdom tradition than as an abstract philosophy.

The early Stoa of Zeno of Citium, Cleanthes, Chrysippus, and Diogenes of Babylon held the beliefs described in this introduction. These beliefs were quite stable from about 300 to 120 BC, with some changes, such as the shift from Zeno's idea that mind is a fiery substance to Chrysippus' idea that mind is fire and air. Diogenes of Babylon is the only early Stoic whose writing is included in this book, though it also includes descriptions of the ideas of Zeno and Chrysippus.

The middle Stoa of Panaetius and Posidonius was more eclectic, willing to modify Stoic beliefs and accept some beliefs from other sources, such as Aristotle. It extends from 120 BC, when Panaetius became scholarch, to 51 BC, when Posidonius died. This book includes a number of selections from Panaetius and Posidonius.

The late Stoa of Epictetus, Seneca, and Marcus Aurelius preserved the Stoic wisdom tradition but did not worry

much about its philosophical ideas. You can see it in the
Meditations of Marcus Aurelius, written in about 170 AD,
almost 500 years after Zeno:

> Begin the morning by saying to thyself, I shall
> meet with the busy-body, the ungrateful, arrogant,
> deceitful, envious, unsocial. All these things
> happen to them by reason of their ignorance of
> what is good and evil. But I who have seen the
> nature of the good that it is beautiful, and of the
> bad that it is ugly, and the nature of him who does
> wrong, that it is akin to me, not only of the same
> blood or seed, but that it participates in the same
> intelligence and the same portion of the divinity, I
> can neither be injured by any of them, for no one
> can fix on me what is ugly, nor can I be angry with
> my kinsman, nor hate him....[22]

Stoicism leads Marcus Aurelius and other late Stoics to make
intensive moral demands on themselves but to accept other
people's flaws as if they were not responsible for them. The
writing of the late Stoa is readily available, though none is
included in this book.

Though it was most successful as a wisdom tradition,
Stoicism also had important philosophical influences. For
example, Stoics invented the ideas of cosmopolitanism and
of natural law, which have been important to our civilization
ever since. Their ethical theory is also important because it
had a strong influence on Antiochus of Ascalon, who was
a major philosopher though he not well known today; his
works can be found in the book *Philosophy of the Syncretic
Academy*.

22 Marcus Aurelius, *The Meditations*, translated by George Long, beginning
of Book II.

Epitome of Zeno's Philosophy
by an unknown doxographer
from *Academica* I: ix-xii

Introduction

In *Academica* Book I, Varro gives a long exposition of the ideas of Antiochus of Ascalon (which is in the book *Philosophy of the Syncretic Academy*), following the conventional division of philosophy into ethics, natural philosophy, and logic. Then he continues with the text given here, a brief transition and a summary of the ideas of Zeno of Citium (c. 334 BC – c. 262 BC), the founder of Stoicism, which follows the same conventional division of philosophy into three parts. Varro is a disciple of Antiochus of Ascalon, and he introduces this section by saying that he will expound Zeno's thinking "as Antiochus used to explain it." But it is not possible that he is still following Antiochus when he talks about Zeno, because he says that Stoic doctrines are substantively different from the doctrines of the Old Academy of Plato and of the Peripatetics, while a key belief of Antiochus was that the Stoics just used different language to state the same doctrines as the Old Academics and the Peripatetics.

When Cicero wrote this dialog, he clearly inserted another work about the Stoics after the work about Antiochus, adding a the transition between the two. Cicero (as a character in the dialog) admits that that this insertion was an error by Cicero (as an author). After Varro finishes, Cicero corrects his claim that the Stoics were substantively different by saying:

> … Antiochus, a great friend of mine, used to assert, that it [Stoicism] is to be considered rather

as a corrected edition of the Old Academy, than as
any new sect.[23]

Judging from its content, this work is by a doxographer,
a writer who summarizes the works of philosophers. Only
fragments of Zeno's own writing survive, and this work
seems to be the best surviving epitome of Zeno's philosophy.

However, this epitome ignores Zeno's writing on
politics: Zeno wrote a book named *Republic* (*Politeia*), which
described an ideal egalitarian Stoic society. By the first
century BC, some Stoics were saying that Zeno had been
"young and thoughtless"[24] when he wrote the *Republic*, so
the omission of Zeno's politics probably dates this work to
the first century BC. Later Stoics developed more respectable
political ideas, as we see in the essay "On Politics" later in
this book.

Cicero's framing of this epitome begins as Varro says to
Cicero (the character in the dialog) that the "Old Academic"
philosophy of Antiochus of Ascalon was the original
philosophy handed down from Plato and was preserved
intact by Plato's successors. This is what Antiochus claimed,
but it is clearly untrue: Antiochus created a new synthesis of
Academic, Peripatetic and Stoic thought, as described in the
introduction to *Philosophy of the Syncretic Academy*.

Cicero's Framing

ix This was the first philosophy handed down to them by
Plato. And if you like I will explain to you those discussions
which have originated in it."

"Indeed," said I, "we shall be glad if you will; and I can
answer for Atticus as well as for myself."

"You are quite right," said he; "for the doctrine both of
the Peripatetics and of the old Academy is most admirably
explained."

"Aristotle, then, was the first to undermine the doctrine

23 *Academica* I: xii.

24 The Epicurean philosopher, Philodemus (c. 110 -. c. 40 or 35 BC),
attributes this view to some Stoics of his time. *On the Stoics*, c. 2. col 9.

of species, which I have just now mentioned, and which Plato had embraced in a wonderful manner; so that he even affirmed that there was something divine in it. But Theophrastus [Aristotle's successor], a man of very delightful eloquence, and of such purity of morals that his probity and integrity were notorious to all men, broke down more vigorously still the authority of the old school; for he stripped virtue of its beauty, and made it powerless, by denying that to live happily depended solely on it. For Strato, his pupil, although a man of brilliant abilities, must still be excluded entirely from that school; for, having deserted that most indispensable part of philosophy which is placed in virtue and morals, and having devoted himself wholly to the investigation of nature, he by that very conduct departs as widely as possible from his companions.

"But Speusippus and Xenocrates, who were the earliest supporters of the system and authority of Plato, — and, after them, Polemo and Crates, and at the same time Crantor — being all collected together in the Academy, diligently maintained those doctrines which they had received from their predecessors.

Zeno's Stoic Philosophy

"Zeno and Arcesilaus had been diligent attenders on Polemo; but Zeno, who preceded Arcesilaus in point of time, and argued with more subtlety, and was a man of the greatest acuteness, attempted to correct the system of that school. And, if you like, I will explain to you the way in which he set about that correction, as Antiochus used to explain it.

"Indeed," said I, I shall be very glad to hear you do so; and you see that Pomponius intimates the same wish."

Zeno on Ethics

x "Zeno, then, was not at all a man like Theophrastus, to cut through the sinews of virtue; but, on the other hand, he was one who placed everything which could have any effect in producing a happy life in virtue alone, and who reckoned nothing else a good at all, and who called that honorable which was single in its nature, and the sole and only good. But as for all other things, although they were neither good nor bad, he divided them, calling some according to, and others contrary to nature. There were others which he looked upon as placed between these two classes, and which he called intermediate. Those which were according to nature, he taught his disciples, deserved to be taken, and to be considered worthy of a certain esteem. To those which were contrary to nature, he assigned a contrary character; and those of the intermediate class he left as neutrals, and attributed to them no importance whatever.

"But of those which he said ought to be taken, he considered some worthy of a higher estimation and others of a less. Those which were worthy of a higher esteem, he called preferred; those which were only worthy of a lower degree, he called rejected. And as he had altered all these things, not so much in fact as in name, so too he defined some actions as intermediate, lying between good deeds and sins, between duty and a violation of duty;—classing things done rightly as good actions, and things done wrongly (that is to say, sins) as bad actions. And several duties, whether discharged or neglected, he considered of an intermediate character, as I have already said.

"And whereas his predecessors had not placed every virtue in reason, but had said that some virtues were perfected by nature, or by habit, he placed them all in reason; and while they thought that those kinds of virtues which I have mentioned above could be separated, he asserted that that could not be done in any manner, and affirmed that not only the practice of virtue (which was the doctrine of his predecessors), but the very disposition to it, was intrinsically beautiful; and that virtue could not possibly be present to any one without his continually practicing it.

"And while they did not entirely remove all perturbation of mind from man, (for they admitted that man did by nature grieve, and desire, and fear, and become elated by joy,) but only contracted it, and reduced it to narrow bounds; he maintained that the wise man was wholly free from all these diseases as they might be called. And as the ancients said that those perturbations were natural, and devoid of reason, and placed desire in one part of the mind and reason in another, he did not agree with them either; for he thought that all perturbations were voluntary, and were admitted by the judgment of the opinion, and that a certain unrestrained intemperance was the mother of all of them. And this is nearly what he laid down about morals.

Zeno on Nature

xi "But about natures he held these opinions. In the first place, he did not connect this fifth nature, out of which his predecessors thought that sense and intellect were produced, with those four principles of things. For he laid it down that fire is that nature which produces everything, and intellect, and sense. But he differed from them again, inasmuch as he thought it absolutely impossible for anything to be produced from that nature which was destitute of body; which was the character attributed by Xenocrates and his predecessors to the mind, and he would not allow that that which produced anything, or which was produced by anything, could possibly be anything except body.

Zeno on Logic (Epistemology)

But he made a great many alterations in that third part of his philosophy, in which, first of all, he said some new things of the senses themselves: which he considered to be united by some impulse as it were, acting upon them from without, which he called *phantasia* and which we may term perception. And let us recollect this word, for we shall have frequent occasion to employ it in the remainder of our discourse; but to these things which are perceived, and as it were accepted by the senses, he adds the assent of the mind, which he considers to be placed in ourselves and voluntary.

"He did not give credit to everything which is perceived, but only to those which contain some especial character of those things which are seen; but he pronounced what was seen, when it was discerned on account of its own power, comprehensible — will you allow me this word?"

"Certainly," said Atticus, for how else are you to express *katalêptos?*"

"But after it had been received and approved, then he called it comprehension, resembling those things which are taken up (*prehenduntur*) in the hand; from which verb also he derived this noun, though no one else had ever used this verb with reference to such matters; and he also used many new words, for he was speaking of new things. But that which was comprehended by sense he called felt (*sensum*), and if it was so comprehended that it could not be eradicated by reason, he called it knowledge; otherwise he called it ignorance: from which also was engendered opinion, which was weak, and compatible with what was false or unknown. But between knowledge and ignorance he placed that comprehension which I have spoken of, and reckoned it neither among what was right or what was wrong, but said that it alone deserved to be trusted.

"And from this he attributed credit also to the senses, because, as I have said above, comprehension made by the senses appeared to him to be true and trustworthy. Not because it comprehended all that existed in a thing, but because it left out nothing which could affect it, and because nature had given it to us to be as it were a rule of knowledge, and a principle from which subsequently all notions of things might be impressed on our minds, from which not only principles, but some broader paths to the discovery of reason are found out. But error, and rashness, and ignorance, and opinion, and suspicion, and in a word everything which was inconsistent with a firm and consistent assent, he discarded from virtue and wisdom.

"And it is in these things that nearly all the disagreement between Zeno and his predecessors, and all his alteration of their system consists."

Cicero's Conclusion

xii And when he had spoken thus—"You have," said I, "O Varro, explained the principles both of the Old Academy and of the Stoics with brevity, but also with great clearness. But I think it to be true, as Antiochus, a great friend of mine, used to assert, that it is to be considered rather as a corrected edition of the Old Academy, than as any new sect."

On the System of Stoic Ethics
by or after Diogenes of Babylon
from *De Finibus* III: i-xxii

Introduction

Cicero's *De Finibus Bonorum et Malorum* (*Of the Ends of Good and Evil*) Book III includes a long discourse by Marcus Cato about the system of Stoic ethics, which is a unified whole that apparently comes from a single source work.

Because this dialog takes place in Cicero's time, the speaker must be Cato the Younger, called Cato of Utica, and not his great-grandfather Cato the Elder, called Cato the Censor. After studying Stoic philosophy, Cato of Utica began living very simply, eating only as much as necessary and subjecting himself to cold and rain. He was a senator, was elected Tribune in 63 BC, and as Tribune, helped Cicero deal with Catiline's conspiracy. He accused Caesar of aiding Catiline, continued to oppose Caesar, and committed suicide in 46 BC rather than losing his freedom by living under Caesar's rule—adding poignancy to his defense of suicide in this discourse. His suicide was so admired that his fame lived on for centuries; Dante made him gatekeeper of the mount of Purgatory, a remarkable honor for a pagan.

Book III begins by referring to earlier books of De Finibus. In Book I, Torquatus defended Epicurean ethics. In Book II, Cicero (the character in the dialog) criticized Epicurean ethics, speaking for the Syncretic Academy of Antiochus of Ascalon, which claimed that there is no difference of substance between Stoic and Peripatetic ethics, just a difference in terminology; this discourse is included in *Philosophy of the Syncretic Academy*. In Book III, after a great deal of gentlemanly conversation, mostly omitted here, Cato gives a long exposition of Stoic ethics.

Cato's discourse is probably based on a text by the Stoic philosopher Diogenes of Babylon (c. 230 – c. 150 to 140 BC), since he mentions Diogenes four times during his discourse as the source of his ideas during his exposition. But he casts a bit of doubt on the source when he says:

> "About good fame ... Chrysippus and Diogenes used to aver that, apart from any practical value it may possess, it is not worth stretching out a finger for; and I strongly agree with them. On the other hand their successors, finding themselves unable to resist the attacks of Carneades, declared that good fame, as I have called it, was preferred and desirable for its own sake...."[25]

This statement obviously does not come from Diogenes himself. It seems possible that Cicero (the author of the book) interjected this remark about later Stoics, but it is also possible that the entire discourse is from some later source work that was based on the ideas of Diogenes of Babylon but was not by him.

Cicero (the character in the dialog) is still speaking for the school of Antiochus of Ascalon in the framing of this work, where he claims that "Zeno their [the Stoics'] founder was rather an inventor of new terms than a discoverer of new ideas."

Cicero's Framing

i ... [Cicero is speaking.] The question before us is, where is that Chief Good, which is the object of our inquiry, to be found? Pleasure we have eliminated; the doctrine that the End of Goods consists in freedom from pain is open to almost identical objections; and in fact no Chief Good could be accepted that was without the element of Virtue, the most excellent thing that can exist.

Hence although in our debate with Torquatus we did not spare our strength, nevertheless a keener struggle now awaits us with the Stoics. For pleasure is a topic that does not lend itself to very subtle or profound discussion; its champions are little skilled in dialectic, and their adversaries have no difficult case to refute. In fact Epicurus himself declares that there is no occasion to argue about pleasure at all: its criterion resides in the senses, so that proof is entirely superfluous; a reminder of the facts is all that is needed. Therefore our preceding debate consisted of a simple statement of the case on either side. There was nothing abstruse or intricate in the discourse of Torquatus, and my own exposition was, I believe, as clear as daylight.

But the Stoics, as you are aware, affect an exceedingly subtle or rather crabbed style of argument; and if the Greeks find it so, still more must we, who have actually to create a vocabulary, and to invent new terms to convey new ideas. This necessity will cause no surprise to anyone of moderate learning, when he reflects that in every branch of science lying outside the range of common everyday practice there must always be a large degree of novelty in the vocabulary, when it comes to fixing a terminology to denote the conceptions with which the science in question deals. Thus Logic and Natural Philosophy alike make use of terms unfamiliar even to Greece; Geometry, Music, Grammar also, have an idiom of their own. Even the manuals of Rhetoric, which belong entirely to the practical sphere and to the life of the world, nevertheless employ for purposes of instruction a sort of private and peculiar phraseology.

ii And to leave out of account these liberal arts and accomplishments, even artisans would be unable to preserve the tradition of their crafts if they did not make use of words unknown to us though familiar to themselves. Nay, agriculture itself, a subject entirely unsusceptible of literary refinement, has yet had to coin technical terms to denote the things with which it is occupied. All the more is the philosopher compelled to do likewise; for philosophy is the Science of Life, and cannot treat its subject in language taken from the street.

Still of all the philosophers the Stoics have been the greatest innovators in this respect, and Zeno their founder was rather an inventor of new terms than a discoverer of new ideas. But if men so learned, using a language generally supposed to be more copious than our own, were allowed in handling recondite subjects to employ unfamiliar terms, how much more right have we to claim this license who are venturing now to approach these topics for the first time? Moreover we have often declared, and this under some protest not from Greeks only but also from persons who would rather be considered Greeks than Romans, that in fullness of vocabulary we are not merely not surpassed by the Greeks but are actually their superiors. We are therefore bound to do our utmost to make good this claim not in our native arts only but also in those that belong to the Greeks themselves. However, words which the practice of past generations permits us to employ as Latin, e.g. the term 'philosophy' itself, or 'rhetoric,' 'logic,' 'grammar,' 'geometry,' 'music' we may consider as being our own; the ideas might it is true have been translated into Latin, but the Greek terms have been familiarized by use. So much for terminology.

…

I was down at my place at Tusculum, and wanted to consult some books from the library of the young Lucullus; so I went to his country-house, as I was in the habit of doing, to help myself to the volumes I needed. On my arrival, seated in the library I found Marcus Cato; I had not known he was there. He was surrounded by piles of books on Stoicism; for he possessed, as you are aware, a voracious appetite for reading, and could never have enough of it; indeed it was often his practice actually to brave the idle censure of the mob by reading in the senate-house itself, while waiting for the senate to assemble, — he did not steal any attention from public business. So it may well be believed that when I found him taking a complete holiday, with a vast supply of books at his command, he had the air of indulging in a literary debauch, if the term may be applied to so honorable an occupation.

…

iii "… How I wish," said he, "that you had thrown in your lot with the Stoics! You of all men might have been expected to reckon virtue as the only good."

"Perhaps you might rather have been expected," I answered, "to refrain from adopting a new terminology, when in substance you think as I do. Our principles agree; it is our language that is at variance."

"Indeed," he rejoined, "they do not agree in the least. Once pronounce anything to be desirable, once reckon anything as a good, other than Moral Worth, and you have extinguished the very light of virtue, Moral Worth itself, and overthrown virtue entirely."

"That all sounds very fine, Cato," I replied, "but are you aware that you share your lofty pretensions with Pyrrho and with Aristo, who make all things equal in value? I should like to know what your opinion is of them."

"My opinion?" he said. "You ask what my opinion is? that those good, brave, just and temperate men, of whom history tells us, or whom we have ourselves seen in our public life, who under the guidance of Nature herself, without the aid of any learning, did many glorious deeds, — that these men were better educated by nature than they could possibly have been by philosophy had they accepted any other system of philosophy than the one that counts Moral Worth the only good and Moral Baseness the only evil. All other philosophical systems — in varying degrees no doubt, but still all, — which reckon anything of which virtue is not an element either as a good or an evil, do not merely, as I hold, give us no assistance or support towards becoming better men, but are actually corrupting to the character. Either this point must be firmly maintained, that Moral Worth is the sole good, or it is absolutely impossible to prove that virtue constitutes happiness. And in that case I do not see why we should trouble to study philosophy. For if anyone who is wise could be miserable, why, I should not set much value on your vaunted and belauded virtue."

iv "What you have said so far, Cato," I answered, "might equally well be said by a follower of Pyrrho or of Aristo. They, as you are aware, think as you do, that this Moral Worth you speak of is not merely the chief but the only Good; and from this of necessity follows the proposition that I notice you maintain, namely, that the Wise are always happy. Do you then," I asked, "commend these philosophers, and think that we ought to adopt this view of theirs?"

"I certainly would not have you adopt their view," he said; "for it is of the essence of virtue to exercise choice among the things in accordance with nature; so that philosophers who make all things absolutely equal, rendering them indistinguishable either as better or worse, and leaving no room for selection among them, have abolished virtue itself."

"Excellently put," I rejoined; "but pray are not you committed to the same position, if you say that only what is right and moral is good, and abolish all distinction between everything else?"

"Quite so," said he, "if I did abolish all distinction, but I do not."

"How so?" I said. "If only virtue, only that one thing which you call moral, right, praiseworthy, becoming (for its nature will be better understood if it is denoted by a number of synonyms), if then, I say, this is the sole good, what other object of pursuit will you have beside it? or, if there be nothing bad but what is base, dishonorable, disgraceful, evil, sinful, foul (to make this clear also by using a variety of terms), what else will you pronounce worthy to be avoided?"

"You know quite well," he retorted, "what I am going to say; but I suspect you want to catch up something in my answer if I put it shortly. So I won't answer you point by point. Instead of that, as we are at leisure, I will expound, unless you think it out of place, the whole system of Zeno and the Stoics."

"Out of place?" I cried. "By no means. Your exposition will be of great assistance towards solving the questions we are asking."

"Then let us make the attempt," said he, "albeit there is a

considerable element of difficulty and obscurity in this Stoic system. For at one time even the terms employed in Greek for its novel conceptions seemed unendurable, when they were novel, though now daily use has made them familiar; what then to you think will be the case in Latin?"

"Do not feel the least difficulty on that score," said I. "If when Zeno invented some novel idea he was permitted to denote it by an equally unheard-of word, why should not Cato be permitted to do so too? Though all the same it need not be a hard and fast rule that every word shall be represented by its exact counterpart, when there is a more familiar word conveying the same meaning. That is the way of a clumsy translator. Indeed my own practice is to use several words to give what is expressed in Greek by one, if I cannot convey the sense other. At the same time I hold that we may fairly claim the license to employ a Greek word when no Latin word is readily forthcoming. Why should this license be granted to *ephippia* (saddles) and *acratophora* (jars for neat wine) more than to *proêgmena* and *apoproêgmena*? These latter however it is true may be correctly translated 'preferred' and 'rejected.' "

"Thanks for your assistance," he said. "I certainly shall use for choice the Latin equivalents you have just given; and in other cases you shall come to my aid if you see me in difficulties."

"I'll do my best," I replied; "but fortune favors the bold, so pray make the venture. What sublimer occupation could we find?"

Primary Impulses of Nature

v He began: "It is the view of those whose system I adopt, that immediately upon birth (for that is the proper point to start from) a living creature feels an attachment for itself, and an impulse to preserve itself and to feel affection for its own constitution and for those things which tend to preserve that constitution; while on the other hand it conceives an antipathy to destruction and to those things which appear to threaten destruction. In proof of this opinion they urge that infants desire things conducive to their health and reject things that are the opposite before they have ever felt pleasure or pain; this would not be the case, unless they felt an affection for their own constitution and were afraid of destruction. But it would be impossible that they should feel desire at all unless they possessed self-consciousness, and consequently felt affection for themselves. This leads to the conclusion that it is love of self which supplies the primary impulse to action.

"Pleasure on the contrary, according to most Stoics, is not to be reckoned among the primary objects of natural impulse; and I very strongly agree with them, for fear lest many immoral consequences would follow if we held that nature has placed pleasure among the earliest objects of desire. But the fact of our affection for the objects first adopted at nature's prompting seems to require no further proof than this, that there is no one who, given the choice, would not prefer to have all the parts of his body sound and whole, rather than maimed or distorted although equally serviceable.

"Again, acts of cognition (which we may term comprehensions or perceptions, or, if these words are distasteful or obscure, *katalêpsis*), — these we consider meet to be adopted for their own sake, because they possess an element that so to speak embraces and contains the truth. This can be seen in the case of children, whom we may observe to take pleasure in finding something out for themselves by the use of reason, even though they gain nothing by it. The sciences also, we consider, are things to be chosen for their own sake, partly because there is in them something worthy of choice, partly because they consist of acts of cognition and contain an element of fact established by methodical reasoning. The mental assent to what is false, as the Stoics believe, is more repugnant to us than all the other things that are contrary to nature.

"Again, of the members or parts of the body, some appear to have been bestowed on us by nature for the sake of their use, for example the hands, legs, feet, and internal organs, as to the degree of whose utility even physicians are not agreed; while others serve no useful purpose, but appear to be intended for ornament: for instance the peacock's tail, the plumage of the dove with its shifting colors, and the breasts and beard of the male human being.

"All this is perhaps somewhat baldly expressed; for it deals with what may be called the primary elements of nature, to which any embellishment of style can scarcely be applied, nor am I for my part concerned to attempt it. On the other hand, when one is treating of more majestic topics the style instinctively rises with the subject, and the brilliance of the language increases with the dignity of the theme."

"True," I rejoined; "but to my mind, any clear statement of an important topic possesses excellence of style. It would be childish to desire an ornate style in subjects of the kind with which you are dealing. A man of sense and education will be content to be able to express his meaning plainly and clearly."

The Valuable

vi "To proceed then," he continued, "for we have been digressing from the primary impulses of nature; and with these the later stages must be in harmony. The next step is the following fundamental classification: That which is in itself in accordance with nature, or which produces something else that is so, and which therefore is deserving of choice as possessing a certain amount of positive value—*axia* as the Stoics call it—this they pronounce to be 'valuable' (for so I suppose we may translate it); and on the other hand that which is the contrary of the former they term 'valueless.'

"The initial principle being thus established that things in accordance with nature are 'things to be taken' for their own sake, and their opposites similarly 'things to be rejected,' the first 'appropriate act' (for so I render the Greek *kathêkon*) is to preserve oneself in one's natural constitution; the next is to retain those things which are in accordance with nature and to repel those that are the contrary; then when this principle of choice and also of rejection has been discovered, there follows next in order choice conditioned by 'appropriate action'; then, such choice become a fixed habit; and finally, choice fully rationalized and in harmony with nature. It is at this final stage that the Good properly so called first emerges and comes to be understood in its true nature.

Moral Worth and Wisdom

"Man's first attraction is towards the things in accordance with nature; but as soon as he has understanding, or rather become capable of 'conception' — in Stoic phraseology *ennoia* — and has discerned the order and so to speak harmony that governs conduct, he thereupon esteems this harmony far more highly than all the things for which he originally felt an affection, and by exercise of intelligence and reason infers the conclusion that herein resides the Chief Good of man, the thing that is praiseworthy and desirable for its own sake; and that inasmuch as this consists in what the Stoics term *homologia* and we with your approval may call 'conformity' — inasmuch I say as in this resides that Good which is the End to which all else is a means, moral conduct and Moral Worth itself, which alone is counted as a good, although of subsequent development, is nevertheless the sole thing that is for its own efficacy and value desirable, whereas none of the primary objects of nature is desirable for its own sake.

"But since those actions which I have termed 'appropriate acts' are based on the primary natural objects, it follows that the former are means to the latter. Hence it may correctly be said that all 'appropriate acts' are means to the end of attaining the primary needs of nature. Yet it must not be inferred that their attainment is the ultimate Good, inasmuch as moral action is not one of the primary natural attractions, but is an outgrowth of these, a later development, as I have said. At the same time moral action is in accordance with nature, and stimulates our desire far more strongly than all the objects that attracted us earlier.

"But at this point a caution is necessary at the outset. It will be an error to infer that this view implies two Ultimate Goods. For though if a man were to make it his purpose to take a true aim with a spear or arrow at some mark, his ultimate end, corresponding to the ultimate good as we pronounce it, would be to do all he could to aim straight: the man in this illustration would have to do everything to aim straight, you yet, although he did everything to attain his purpose, his 'ultimate End,' so to speak, would be what corresponded to what we call the Chief Good in the conduct of life, whereas the actual hitting of the mark would be in our phrase 'to be chosen' but not 'to be desired.'

vii "Again, as all 'appropriate acts' are based on the primary impulses of nature, it follows that Wisdom itself is based on them also. But as it often happens that a man who is introduced to another values this new friend more highly than he does the person who gave him the introduction, so in like manner it is by no means surprising that though we are first commended to Wisdom by the primary natural instincts, afterwards Wisdom itself becomes dearer to us than are the instincts from which we came to her.

"And just as our limbs are so fashioned that it is clear that they were bestowed upon us with a view to a certain mode of life, so our faculty of appetition, in Greek *hormê*, was obviously designed not for any kind of life one may choose, but for a particular mode of living; and the same is true of Reason and of perfected Reason. For just as an actor or dancer has assigned to him not any but a certain particular part or dance, so life has to be conducted in a certain fixed way, and not in any way we like. This fixed way we speak of as 'conformable' and suitable. In fact we do not consider Wisdom to be like seamanship or medicine, but rather like the arts of acting and of dancing just mentioned; its End, being the actual exercise of the art, is contained within the art itself, and is not something extraneous to it.

"At the same time there is also another point which marks

a dissimilarity between Wisdom and these arts as well. In the latter a movement perfectly executed nevertheless does not involve all the various motions which together constitute the subject matter of the art; whereas in the sphere of conduct, what we may call, if you approve, 'right actions,' or 'rightly performed actions,' in Stoic phraseology *katorthōmata*, contain all the factors of virtue. For Wisdom alone is entirely self-contained, which is not the case with the other arts.

"It is erroneous, however, to place the End of medicine or of navigation exactly on a par with the End of Wisdom. For Wisdom includes also magnanimity and justice and a sense of superiority to all the accidents of man's estate, but this is not the case with the other arts. Again, even the very virtues I have just mentioned cannot be attained by anyone unless he has realized that all things are indifferent and indistinguishable except moral worth and baseness.

Moral Worth as the Only Good

"We may now observe how strikingly the principles I have established support the following corollaries. Inasmuch as the final aim — (and you have observed, no doubt, that I have all along been translating the Greek term *telos* either by 'final' or 'ultimate aim,' or 'chief Good,' and for 'final or ultimate aim' we may also substitute 'End') — inasmuch then as the final aim is to live in agreement and harmony with nature, it necessarily follows that all wise men at all times enjoy a happy, perfect and fortunate life, free from all hindrance, interference or want. The essential principle not merely of the system of philosophy I am discussing but also of our life and destinies is, that we should believe Moral Worth to be the only good. This principle might be amplified and elaborated in the rhetorical manner, with great length and fullness and with all the resources of choice diction and impressive argument; but for my own part I like the concise and pointed 'consequences' of the Stoics.

viii "They put their arguments in the following syllogistic

form: Whatever is good is praiseworthy; but whatever is praiseworthy is morally honorable: therefore that which is good is morally honorable. Does this seem to you a valid deduction? Surely it must: you can see that the conclusion consists in what necessarily resulted from the two premises. The usual line of reply is to deny the major premise, and say that not everything good is praiseworthy; for there is no denying that what is praiseworthy is morally honorable. But it would be paradoxical to maintain that there is something good which is not desirable; or desirable that is not pleasing; or if pleasing, not also esteemed; and therefore approved as well; and so also praiseworthy. But the praiseworthy is the morally honorable. Hence it follows that what is good is also morally honorable.

"Next I ask, who can be proud of a life that is miserable or not happy? It follows that one can only be proud of one's lot when it is a happy one. This proves that the happy life is a thing that deserves (so to put it) that one should be proud of it; and this cannot rightly be said of any life but one morally honorable. Therefore the moral life is the happy life. And the man who deserves and wins praise has exceptional cause for pride and self-satisfaction; but these things count for so much that he can justly be pronounced happy; therefore the life of such a man can with full correctness be described as happy also. Thus if Moral Worth is the criterion of happiness, Moral Worth must be deemed the only Good.

"Once more; could it be denied that it is impossible for there ever to exist a man of steadfast, firm and lofty mind, such a one as we call a brave man, unless it be established that pain is not an evil? For just as it is impossible for one who counts death as an evil not to fear death, so in no case can a man disregard and despise a thing that he decides to be evil. This being laid down as generally admitted, we take as our minor premise that the brave and high-minded man despises and holds of no account all the accidents to which mankind is liable. The conclusion follows that nothing is evil that is not base. Also, your lofty, distinguished, magnanimous and truly brave man, who thinks all human vicissitudes beneath him, I mean, the character we desire to produce, our ideal man, must unquestionably have faith in himself and in his own character both past and future, and think well of himself, holding that no ill can befall the wise man. Here then is another proof of the same position, that Moral Worth alone is good, and that to live honorably, that is virtually, is to live happily.

ix "I am well aware, it is true, that varieties of opinion have existed among philosophers, I mean among those of them who have placed the Chief Good, the ultimate aim as I call it, in the mind. Some of those who adopted this view fell into error; but nevertheless I rank all those, of whatever type, who have placed the Chief Good in the mind and in virtue, not merely above the three philosophers who dissociate the Chief Good from virtue altogether and identified it either with pleasure or freedom from pain or the primary impulses of nature, but also above the other three, who held that virtue would be incomplete without some enhancement, and therefore added to it one or other respectively of the three things I have just enumerated. But still those thinkers are quite beside the mark who pronounced the ultimate Good to be a life devoted to knowledge; and those who declared that all things are indifferent, and that the Wise Man will secure happiness by not preferring any one thing in the least degree to any other; and those again who said, as some members of the Academy are said to have maintained, that the final Good and supreme duty of the Wise Man is to resist appearances and resolutely withhold his assent to the reality of sense-impressions. It is customary to take these doctrines severally and reply to them at length. But there is really no need to labor what is self-evident; and what could be more obvious than that, if we can exercise no choice as between things consonant with and things contrary to nature, the much-prized and belauded virtue of Prudence is abolished altogether?

"Eliminating therefore the views just enumerated and any others that resemble them, we are left with the conclusion that the Chief Good consists in applying to the conduct of life a knowledge of the working of natural causes, choosing what is in accordance with nature and rejecting what is contrary to it; in other words, the Chief Good is to live in agreement and in harmony with nature.

"But in the other arts when we speak of an 'artistic' performance, this quality must be considered as in a sense subsequent to and a result of the action; it is what the Stoics term *epigennêmatikon* (in the nature of an after-growth). Whereas in conduct, when we speak of an act as 'wise,' the term is applied with full correctness from the first inception of the act. For every action that the Wise Man initiates must necessarily be complete forthwith in all its parts; since the thing desirable, as we term it, consists in his activity. As it is a sin to betray one's country, to use violence to one's parents, to rob a temple, where the offence lies in the result of the act, so the passions of fear, grief and lust are sins, even when no extraneous result ensues. The latter are sins not in their subsequent effects, but immediately upon their inception; similarly, actions springing from virtue are to be judged right from their first inception, and not in their successful completion.

x "Again, the term 'Good,' which has been employed so frequently in this discourse, is also explained by definition. The Stoic definitions do indeed differ from one another in a very minute degree, but they all point in the same direction. Personally I agree with Diogenes in defining the Good as that which is by nature perfect. He was led by this also to pronounce the 'beneficial' (for so let us render the Greek *ōphelêma*) to be a motion or state in accordance with that which is by nature perfect.

"Now notions of things are produced in the mind when something has become known either by experience or combination of ideas or analogy or logical inference. The mind ascends by inference from the things in accordance with nature till finally it arrives at the notion of Good. At the same time Goodness is absolute, and is not a question of degree; the Good is recognized and pronounced to be good from its own inherent properties and not by comparison with other things. Just as honey, though extremely sweet, is yet perceived to be sweet by its own peculiar kind of flavor and not by being compared with something else, so this Good which we are discussing is indeed superlatively valuable, yet its value depends on kind and not on quantity. Value, in Greek *axia*, is not counted as a Good nor yet as an Evil; so that however much you increase it in amount, it will still remain the same in kind. The value of Virtue is therefore peculiar and distinct; it depends on kind and not on degree.

"Moreover the emotions of the mind, which harass and embitter the life of the foolish (the Greek term for these is *pathos*, and I might have rendered this literally and styled them 'diseases,' but the word 'disease' would not suit all instances; for example, no one speaks of pity, nor yet anger, as a disease, though the Greeks term these *pathos*. Let us then accept the term 'emotion,' the very sound of which seems to denote something vicious, and these emotions are not excited by any natural influence. The list of the emotions is divided into four classes, with numerous subdivisions, namely sorrow, fear, lust, and that mental emotion which the Stoics call by a name that also denotes a bodily feeling, *hêdonê* 'pleasure,' but which I prefer to style 'delight,' meaning the sensuous elation of the mind when in a state of exaltation), these emotions, I say, are not excited by any influence of nature; they are all of them mere fancies and frivolous opinions. Therefore the Wise Man will always be free from them.

xi "The view that all Moral Worth is intrinsically desirable is one that we hold in common with many other systems of philosophy. Excepting three schools that shut out Virtue from the Chief Good altogether, all the remaining philosophers are committed to this opinion, and most of all the Stoics, with whom we are now concerned, and who hold that nothing else but Moral Worth is to be counted as a good at all. But this position is one that is extremely simple and easy to defend. For who is there, or who ever was there, of avarice so consuming and appetites so unbridled, that, even though willing to commit any crime to achieve his end, and even though absolutely secure of impunity, yet would not a hundred times rather attain the same object by innocent than by guilty means?

"Again, what desire for profit or advantage underlies our curiosity to learn the secrets of nature, the mode and the causes of the movements of the heavenly bodies? Who lives in such a boorish state, or who has become so rigidly insensible to natural impulses, as to feel a repugnance for these lofty studies and eschew them as valueless apart from any pleasure or profit they may bring? Or who is there who feels no sense of pleasure when he hears of the wise words and brave deeds of our forefathers, — of the Africani, or my great-grandfather whose name is always on your lips, and the other heroes of valor and of virtue? On the other hand, what man of honorable family and good breeding and education is not shocked by moral baseness as such, even when it is not calculated to do him personally any harm? who can view without disgust a person whom he believes to be dissolute and an evil liver? who does not hate the mean, the empty, the frivolous, the worthless?

"Moreover, if we decide that baseness is not a thing to be avoided for its own sake, what arguments can be urged against men's indulging in every sort of unseemliness in privacy and under cover of darkness, unless they are deterred by the essential and intrinsic ugliness of what is base? Endless reasons could be given in support of this view, but they are not necessary. For nothing is less open to doubt than that what is morally good is to be desired for its own sake, and similarly what is morally bad is to be avoided for its own sake.

"Again, the principle already discussed, that Moral Worth is the sole Good, involves the corollary that it is of more value than those neutral things which it procures. On the other hand when we say that folly, cowardice, injustice and intemperance are to be avoided because of the consequences they entail, this dictum must not be so construed as to appear inconsistent with the principle already laid down, that moral baseness alone is evil; for the reason that the consequences referred to are not a matter of bodily harm but of the base conduct to which vices give rise (the term 'vice' I prefer to 'badness' as a translation of the Greek *kakia*)."

xii "Indeed, Cato," said I, "your language is lucidity itself; it conveys your meaning exactly. In fact I feel you are teaching philosophy to speak Latin, and naturalizing her as a Roman citizen. Hitherto she has seemed a foreigner at Rome, and shy of conversing in our language; and this is especially so with your Stoic system because of its precision and subtlety alike of thought and language. (There are some philosophers, I know, who could express their ideas in any language; for they ignore Division and Definition altogether, and themselves profess that they only seek to commend doctrines to which nature assents without argument. Hence, their ideas being so far from recondite, they spend small pains on logical exposition.) So I am following you attentively, and am committing to memory all the terms you use to denote the conceptions we are discussing; for very likely I shall soon have to employ the same terms myself. Well, I think you are quite correct in calling the opposite of the virtues 'vices.' This is in conformity with the usage of our language. The word 'vice' denotes, I believe, that which is in its own nature 'vituperable'; or else 'vituperable' is derived from 'vice.' Whereas if you had rendered *kakia* by 'badness' ('malice'), Latin usage would point us to another meaning, that of a single particular vice. As it is, we make 'vice' the opposite term to 'virtue' in general."

Difference from Peripatetics

"Well, then," resumed Cato, "these principles established there follows a great dispute, which on the side of the Peripatetics was carried on with no great pertinacity (in fact their ignorance of logic renders their habitual style of discourse somewhat deficient in cogency); but your leader Carneades [of the skeptical Academy] with his exceptional proficiency in logic and his consummate eloquence brought the controversy to a head. Carneades never ceased to contend that on the whole so-called 'problem of good and evil,' there was no disagreement as to facts between the Stoics and the Peripatetics, but only as to terms. For my part, however, nothing seems to me more manifest than that there is more of a real than a verbal difference of opinion between those philosophers on these points. I maintain that there is a far greater discrepancy between the Stoics and the Peripatetics as to facts than as to words. The Peripatetics say that all the things which under their system are called goods contribute to happiness; whereas our school does not believe that total happiness comprises everything that deserves to have a certain amount of value attached to it.

xiii "Again, can anything be more certain than that on the theory of the school that counts pain as an evil, the Wise Man cannot be happy when he is being tortured on the rack? Whereas the system that considers pain no evil clearly proves that the Wise Man retains his happiness amidst the worst torments. The mere fact that men endure the same pain more easily when they voluntarily undergo it for the sake of their country than when they suffer it for some lesser cause, shows that the intensity of the pain depends on the state of mind of the sufferer, not on its own intrinsic nature.

"Further, on the Peripatetic theory that there are three kinds of goods, the more abundantly supplied a man is with bodily or external goods, the happier he is; but it does not follow that we Stoics can accept the same position, and say that the more a man has of those bodily things that are highly valued the happier he is. For the Peripatetics hold that the sum of happiness includes bodily advantages, but we deny this altogether. We hold that the multiplication even of those goods that in our view are truly so called does not render life happier or more desirable or of higher value; even less therefore is happiness affected by the accumulation of bodily advantages. Clearly if wisdom and health be both desirable, a combination of the two would be more desirable than wisdom alone; but it is not the case that if both be deserving of value, wisdom plus health is worth more than wisdom by itself separately. We deem health to be deserving of a certain value, but we do not reckon it a good; at the same time we rate no value so highly as to place it above virtue. This is not the view of the Peripatetics, who are bound to say that an action which is both morally good and not attended by pain is more desirable than the same action if accompanied by pain. We think otherwise — whether rightly or wrongly, I will consider later; but how could there be a wider or more real difference of opinion?

xiv "The light of a lamp is eclipsed and overpowered by the rays of the sun; a drop of honey is lost in the vastness of the Aegean sea; an additional sixpence is nothing amid the wealth of Croesus, or a single step in the journey from here to India. Similarly if the Stoic definition of the End of Goods be accepted, it follows that all the value you set on bodily advantages must be absolutely eclipsed and annihilated by the brilliance and the majesty of virtue. And just as opportuneness (for so let us translate *eukairia*) is not increased by prolongation in time (since things we call opportune have attained their proper measure), so right conduct (for thus I translate *katorthōsis*, since *katorthōma* is a single right action), right conduct, I say, and also propriety, and lastly Good itself, which consists in harmony with nature, are not capable of increase or addition. For these things that I speak of, like opportuneness before mentioned, are not made greater by prolongation.

"And on this ground the Stoics do not deem happiness to be any more attractive or desirable if it be lasting than if it be brief; and they use this illustration: Just as, supposing the merit of a shoe were to fit the foot, many shoes would not be superior to few shoes nor bigger shoes to smaller ones, so, in the case of things the good of which consists solely and entirely in propriety and opportuneness, a larger number of these things will not be rated higher than a smaller number nor those lasting longer to those of shorter duration.

Nor is there much point in the argument that, if good health is more valuable when lasting than when brief, therefore the exercise of wisdom also is worth most when it continues longest. This ignores the fact that, whereas the value of health is estimated by duration, that of virtue is measured by opportuneness; so that those who use the argument in question might equally be expected to say that an easy death or an easy child-birth would be better if protracted than if speedy. They fail to see that some things are rendered more valuable by brevity as others by prolongation.

"So it would be consistent with the principles already stated that on the theory of those who deem the End of Goods, that which we term the extreme or ultimate Good, to be capable of degree, they should also hold that one man can be wiser than another, and similarly that one can commit a more sinful or more righteous action than another; which it is not open for us to say, who do not think that the end of Goods can vary in degree. For just as a drowning man is no more able to breathe if he be not far from the surface of the water, so that he might at any moment emerge, than if he were actually at the bottom already, and just as a puppy on the point of opening its eyes is no less blind than one just born, similarly a man that has made some progress towards the state of virtue is none the less in misery than he that has made no progress at all.

xv "I am aware that all this seems paradoxical; but as our previous conclusions are undoubtedly true and well established, and as these are the logical inferences from them, the truth of these inferences also cannot be called in question. Yet although the Stoics deny that either virtues or vices can be increased in degree, they nevertheless believe that each of them can be in a sense expanded and widened in scope.

Wealth again, in the opinion of Diogenes [of Babylon], though so important for pleasure and health as to be not merely conducive but actually essential to them, yet has not the same effect in relation to virtue, nor yet in the case of the other arts; for money may be a guide to these, but cannot form an essential factor in them; therefore although if pleasure or if good health be a good, wealth also must be counted a good, yet if wisdom is a good, it does not follow that we must also pronounce wealth to be a good. Nor can thing which is not a good be essential to a thing that is a good; and hence, because acts of cognition and of comprehension, which form the raw material of the arts, excite desire, since wealth is not a good, wealth cannot be essential to any art. But even if we allowed wealth to be essential to the arts, the same argument nevertheless could not be applied to virtue, because virtue (as Diogenes argues) requires a great amount of thought and practice, which is not the case to the same extent with the arts, and because virtue involves life-long steadfastness, strength and consistency, whereas these qualities are not equally manifested in the arts.

Good versus Valuable

"Next follows an exposition of the difference between things; for if we maintained that all things were absolutely indifferent, the whole of life would be thrown into confusion, as it is by Aristo, and no function or task could be found for wisdom, since there would be absolutely no distinction between the things that pertain to the conduct of life, and no choice need be exercised among them. Accordingly after conclusively proving that morality alone is good and baseness alone evil, the Stoics went on to affirm that among those things which were of no importance for happiness or misery, there was nevertheless an element of difference, making some of them of positive and others of negative value, and others neutral. Again among things valuable — e.g. health, unimpaired senses, freedom from pain, fame, wealth and the like — they said that some afford us adequate grounds for preferring them to other things, while others are not of this nature; and similarly among those things which are of negative value some afford adequate grounds for our rejecting them, such as pain, disease, loss of the senses, poverty, disgrace, and the like; others not so. Hence arose the distinction, in Zeno's terminology, between *proêgmena* and the opposite, *apoproêgmena* — for Zeno using the copious Greek language still employed novel words coined for the occasion, a license not allowed to us with the poor vocabulary of Latin; though you are fond of saying that Latin is actually more copious than Greek. However, to make it easier to understand the meaning of this term it will not be out of place to explain the method which Zeno pursued in coining it.

xvi "In a royal court, Zeno remarks, no one speaks of the king himself as 'promoted' to honor (for that is the meaning of *proêgmenon*), but the term is applied to those holding some office of state whose rank most nearly approaches, though it is second to, the royal preeminence; similarly in the conduct of life the title *proêgmenon*, that is, 'promoted,' is to be given not to those things which are in the first rank, but to those which hold the second place; for these we may use either the term suggested (for that will be a literal translation) or 'advanced' and 'degraded,' or the term we have been using all along, 'preferred' or 'superior,' and for the opposite 'rejected.' If the meaning is intelligible we need not be punctilious about the use of words.

"But since we declare that everything that is good occupies the first rank, it follows that this which we entitle preferred or superior is neither good nor evil; and accordingly we define it as being indifferent but possessed of a moderate value — since it has occurred to me that I may use the word 'indifferent' to represent their term *adiaphoron*. For in fact, it was inevitable that the class of intermediate things should contain some things that were either in accordance with nature, or the reverse, and this being so, that this class should include some things which possessed moderate value, and, granting this, that some things of this class should be 'preferred.' There were good grounds therefore for making this distinction; and furthermore, to elucidate the matter still more clearly they put forward the following illustration: Just as, supposing we were to assume that our end and aim is to throw a knuckle-bone in such a way that it may stand upright, a bone that is thrown so as to fall upright will be in some measure 'preferred' or advanced' in relation to the proposed end, and one that falls otherwise the reverse, and yet that 'advance' on the part of the knuckle-bone will not be a constituent part of the end indicated, so those things which are 'preferred' are it is true means to the End but are in no sense constituents of its essential nature.

"Next comes the division of goods into three classes, first those which are 'constituents' of the final end (for so I represent the term *telika*, this being a case of an idea which we may decide, as we agreed, to express in several words as we cannot do so in one, in order to make the meaning clear), secondly those which are 'productive' of the End, the Greek *poiêtika*; and thirdly those which are both. The only instances of goods of the 'constituent' class are moral action; the only instance of a 'productive' good is a friend. Wisdom, according to the Stoics, is both constituent and productive; for as being itself an appropriate activity it comes under what I called the constituent class; as causing and producing moral actions, it can be called productive.

xvii "These things which we call 'preferred' are in some cases preferred for their own sake, in others because they produce a certain result, and in others for both reasons; for their own sake, as a certain cast of features and of countenance, or a certain pose or movement, things which may be in themselves either preferable or to be rejected; others will be called preferred because they produce a certain result, for example, money; others again for both reasons, like sound senses and good health. About good fame (that term being a better translation in this context than 'glory' of the Stoic expression *eudoxia*) Chrysippus and Diogenes used to aver that, apart from any practical value it may possess, it is not worth stretching out a finger for; and I strongly agree with them. On the other hand their successors, finding themselves unable to resist the attacks of Carneades, declared that good fame, as I have called it, was preferred and desirable for its own sake, and that a man of good breeding and liberal education would desire to have the good opinion of his parents and relatives, and of good men in general, and that for its own sake and not for any practical advantage; and they argue that just as we desire the welfare of our children, even of such as may be born after we are dead, for their own sake, so a man ought to study his reputation even after death, for itself, even apart from any advantage.

"But although we pronounce Moral Worth to be the sole good, it is nevertheless consistent to perform an appropriate act, in spite of the fact that we count appropriate action neither a good nor an evil. For in the sphere of these neutral things there is an element of reasonableness, in the sense that an account can be rendered of it, and therefore in the sense that an account can also be rendered of its performance; and this proves that an appropriate act is an intermediate thing, to be reckoned neither as a good nor as the opposite. And since those things which are neither to be counted among virtues nor vices nevertheless contain a factor which can be useful, their element of utility is worth preserving. Again, this neutral class also includes action of a certain kind, viz. such that reason calls upon us to do or to produce some one of these neutral things; but an action reasonably performed we call an appropriate act; appropriate action therefore is included in the class which is reckoned neither as good nor the opposite.

xviii "It is also clear that some actions are performed by the Wise Man in the sphere of these neutral things. Well then, when he does such an action he judges it to be an appropriate act. And as his judgment on this point never errs, therefore appropriate action will exist in the sphere of these neutral things. The same thing is also proved by the following argument: We observe that something exists which we call right action; but this is an appropriate act perfectly performed; therefore there will also be such a thing as an imperfect appropriate act; so that, if to restore a trust as a matter of principle is a right act, to restore a trust must be counted as an appropriate act; the addition of the qualification 'on principle' makes it a right action: the mere restitution in itself is counted an appropriate act. Again, since there can be no question but that class of things we call neutral includes some things worthy to be chosen and others to be rejected; therefore whatever is done or described in this manner is entirely included under the term appropriate action. "This shows that since love of self is implanted by nature in all men, both the foolish and the wise alike will choose what is in accordance with nature and reject the contrary. Thus there is a region of appropriate action which is common to the wise and the unwise; and this proves that appropriate action deals with the things we call neutral.

"But since these neutral things form the basis of all appropriate acts, there is good ground for the dictum that it is with these things that all our practical deliberations deal, including the will to live and the will to quit this life. When a man's circumstances contain a preponderance of things in accordance with nature, it is appropriate for him to remain alive; when he possesses or sees in prospect a majority of the contrary things, it is appropriate for him to depart from life. This makes it plain that it is on occasion appropriate for the Wise Man to quit life although he is happy, and also of the Foolish Man to remain in life although he is miserable. For with the Stoics good and evil, as has repeatedly been said already, are a subsequent outgrowth; whereas the primary things of nature, whether favorable or the reverse, fall under the judgment and choice of the Wise Man, and form so to speak the subject-matter, the given material with which wisdom deals. Therefore the reasons both for remaining in life and for departing from it are to be measured entirely by the primary things of nature aforesaid. For the virtuous man is not necessarily retained in life by virtue, and also those who are devoid of virtue need not necessarily seek death.

"And very often it is appropriate for the Wise Man to abandon life at a moment when he is enjoying supreme happiness, if an opportunity offers for making a timely exit. For the Stoic view is that happiness, which means life in harmony with nature, is a matter of seizing the right moment. So that Wisdom her very self upon occasion bids the Wise Man to leave her.

"Hence, as vice does not possess the power of furnishing a reason for suicide, it is clear that even for the foolish, who are also miserable, it is appropriate to remain alive if they possess a predominance of those things which we pronounce to be in accordance with nature. And since the fool is equally miserable when departing from life and when remaining in it, and the undesirability of his life is not increased by its prolongation, there is good ground for saying that those who are in a position to enjoy a preponderance of things that are natural ought to remain in life.

Natural Impulse to Society

xix "Again, it is held by the Stoics to be important to understand that nature creates in parents an affection for their children; and parental affection is the source to which we trace the origin of the association of the human race in communities. This cannot but be clear in the first place from the conformation of the body and its members, which by themselves are enough to show that nature's scheme included the procreation of offspring. Yet it could not be consistent that nature should at once intend offspring to be born and make no provision for that offspring when born to be loved and cherished. Even in the lower animals nature's operation can be clearly discerned; when we observe the labor that they spend on bearing and rearing their young, we seem to be listening to the actual voice of nature. Hence as it is manifest that it is natural for us to shrink from pain, so it is clear that we derive from nature herself the impulse to love those to whom we have given birth.

"From this impulse is developed the sense of mutual attraction which unites human beings as such; this also is bestowed by nature. The mere fact of their common humanity requires that one man should feel another man to be akin to him. For just as some of the parts of the body, such as the eyes and the ears, are created as it were for their own sakes, while others like the legs or the hands also subserve the utility of the rest of the members, so some very large animals are born for themselves alone; whereas the sea-pen, as it is called, in its roomy shell, and the creature named the 'pinoteres' because it keeps watch over the sea-pen, which swims out of the sea-pen's shell, then retires back into it and is shut up inside, thus appearing to have warned its host to be on its guard — these creatures, and also the ant, the bee, the stork, do certain actions for the sake of others besides themselves. With human beings this bond of mutual aid is far more intimate. It follows that we are by nature fitted to form unions, societies and states.

"Again, they hold that the universe is governed by divine will; it is a city or state of which both men and gods are members, and each one of us is a part of this universe; from which it is a natural consequence that we should prefer the common advantage to our own. For just as the laws set the safety of all above the safety of individuals, so a good, wise and law-abiding man, conscious of his duty to the state, studies the advantage of all more than that of himself or of any single individual. The traitor to his country does not deserve greater reprobation than the man who betrays the common advantage or security for the sake of his own advantage or security. This explains why praise is owed to one who dies for the commonwealth, because it becomes us to love our country more than ourselves. And as we feel it wicked and inhuman for men to declare (the saying is usually expressed in a familiar Greek line) that they care not if, when they themselves are dead, the universal conflagration ensues, it is undoubtedly true that we are bound to study the interest of posterity also for its own sake.

xx "This is the feeling that has given rise to the practice of making a will and appointing guardians for one's children when one is dying. And the fact that no one would care to pass his life alone in a desert, even though supplied with pleasures in unbounded profusion, readily shows that we are born for society and intercourse, and for a natural partnership with our fellow men.

"Moreover nature inspires us with the desire to benefit

as many people as we can, and especially by imparting information and the principles of wisdom. Hence it would be hard to discover anyone who will not impart to another any knowledge that he may himself possess; so strong is our propensity not only to learn but also to teach. And just as bulls have a natural instinct to fight with all their strength and force in defending their calves against lions, so men of exceptional gifts and capacity for service, like Hercules and Liber in the legends, feel a natural impulse to be the protectors of the human race. Also when we confer upon Jove the titles of Most Good and Most Great, of Savior, Lord of Guests, Rallier of Battles, what we mean to imply is that the safety of mankind lies in his keeping. But how inconsistent it would be for us to expect the immortal gods to love and cherish us, when we ourselves despise and neglect one another! Therefore just as we actually use our limbs before we have learnt for what particular useful purpose they were bestowed upon us, so we are united and allied by nature in the common society of the state. Were this not so, there would be no room either for justice or benevolence.

"But just as they hold that man is united with man by the bonds of right, so they consider that no right exists as between man and beast. For Chrysippus well said, that all other things were created for the sake of men and gods, but that these exist for their own mutual fellowship and society, so that men can make use of beasts for their own purposes without injustice. And the nature of man, he said, is such, that as it were a code of law subsists between the individual and the human race, so that he who upholds this code will be just and he who departs from it, unjust. But just as, though the theatre is a public place, yet it is correct to say that the particular seat a man has taken belongs to him, so in the state or in the universe, though these are common to all, no principle of justice militates against the possession of private property.

"Again, since we see that man is designed by nature to safeguard and protect his fellows, it follows from this natural disposition, that the Wise Man should desire to engage in politics and government, and also to live in accordance with nature by taking to himself a wife and desiring to have children by her. Even the passion of love when pure is not thought incompatible with the character of the Stoic sage. As for the principles and habits of the Cynics, some say that these befit the Wise Man, if circumstances should happen to indicate this course of action; but other Stoics reject the Cynic rule unconditionally.

xxi "To safeguard the universal alliance, solidarity and affection that subsist between man and man, the Stoics held that both 'benefits' and 'injuries' (in their terminology, *ōphelêmata* and *blammata*) are common, the former doing good and the latter harm; and they pronounce them to be not only 'common' but also 'equal.' 'Disadvantages' and 'advantages' (for so I render *euchrêstêmata* and *duschrêstêmata*) they held to be 'common' but not 'equal.' For things 'beneficial' and 'injurious' are goods and evils respectively, and these must needs be equal; but 'advantages' and 'disadvantages' belong to the class we speak of as 'preferred' and 'rejected,' and these may differ in degree. But whereas 'benefits' and 'injuries' are pronounced to be 'common,' righteous and sinful acts are not considered 'common.'

"They recommend the cultivation of friendship, classing it among 'things beneficial.' In friendship some profess that the Wise Man will hold his friends' interests as dear as his own, while others say that a man's own interests must necessarily be dearer to him; at the same time the latter admit that to enrich oneself by another's loss is an action repugnant to that justice towards which we seem to possess a natural propensity. But the school I am discussing emphatically rejects the view that we adopt or approve either justice or friendship for the sake of their utility. For if it were so, the same claims of utility would be able to undermine and overthrow them. In fact the very existence of both justice and friendship will be impossible if they are not desired for their own sake.

"Right moreover, properly so styled and entitled, exists (they aver) by nature; and it is foreign to the nature of the

Wise Man not only to wrong but even to hurt anyone. Nor again is it righteous to enter into a partnership in wrongdoing with one's friends or benefactors; and it is most truly and cogently maintained that honesty is always the best policy, and that whatever is fair and just is also honorable, and conversely whatever is honorable will also be just and fair.

Conclusion of the Work

"To the virtues we have discussed they also add Dialectic and Natural Philosophy. Both of these they entitle by the name of virtue; the former because it conveys a method that guards us for giving assent to any falsehood or ever being deceived by specious probability, and enables us to retain and to defend the truths that we have learned about good and evil; for without the art of Dialectic they hold that any man may be seduced from truth into error. If therefore rashness and ignorance are in all matters fraught with mischief, the art which removes them is correctly entitled a virtue.

xxii "The same honor is also bestowed with good reason upon Natural Philosophy, because he who is to live in accordance with nature must base his principles upon the system and government of the entire world. Nor again can anyone judge truly of things good and evil, save by a knowledge of the whole plan of nature and also of the life of the gods, and of the answer to the question whether the nature of man is or is not in harmony with that of the universe. And no one without Natural Philosophy can discern the value (and their value is very great) of the ancient maxims and precepts of the Wise Men, such as to 'obey occasion,' 'follow God,' 'know thyself,' and 'moderation in all things.' Also this science alone can impart a conception of the power of nature in fostering justice and maintaining friendship and the rest of the affections; nor again without unfolding nature's secrets can we understand the sentiment of piety towards the gods or the degree of gratitude that we owe to them.

"However I begin to perceive that I have let myself be carried beyond the requirements of the plan that I set before me. The fact is that I have been led on by the marvelous structure of the Stoic system and the miraculous sequence of its topics; pray tell me seriously, does it not fill you with admiration? Nothing is more finished, more nicely ordered, than nature; but what has nature, what have the products of handicraft to show that is so well constructed, so firmly jointed and welded into one? Where do you find a conclusion inconsistent with its premise, or a discrepancy between an earlier and a later statement? Where is lacking such close interconnection of the parts that, if you alter a single letter, you shake the whole structure? Though indeed there is nothing that it would be possible to alter.

"Then, how dignified, how lofty, how consistent is the character of the Wise Man as they depict it! Since reason has proved that moral worth is the sole good, it follows that he must always be happy, and that all those titles which the ignorant are so fond of deriding do in very truth belong to him. ... Rightly will he be said to own all things, who alone knows how to use all things; rightly also will he be styled beautiful, for the features of the soul are fairer than those of the body; rightly the one and only free man, as subject to no man's authority, and slave of no appetite; rightly unconquerable, for though his body be thrown into fetters, no bondage can enchain his soul. Nor need he wait for any period of time, that the decision whether he has been happy or not may be finally pronounced only when he has rounded off his life's last day in death, — the famous warning so unwisely given to Croesus by old Solon, one of the seven Wise Men; for had Croesus ever been happy, he would have carried his happiness uninterrupted to the pyre raised for him by Cyrus.

"If then it be true that all the good and none but the good are happy, what possession is more precious than philosophy, what more divine than virtue?"

Five Stoic Works on Theology and Nature
from *De Natura Deorum* II: i-lxvi

Introduction

Book II of *De Natura Deorum* (*Of the Nature of the Gods*) is a discourse defending the Stoic view of theology and nature delivered by Quintus Lucilius Balbus, who was himself a Stoic philosopher who studied under Panaetius and who lived in Cadiz, Spain.

Balbus begins by stating his plan for the whole discourse: "the topic of the immortal gods which you raise is divided by our school into four parts: first they prove that the gods exist; next they explain their nature; then they show that the world is governed by them; and lastly that they care for the fortunes of mankind." His discourse generally follows this plan, but the four parts clearly have been taken from four different treatises and have not been edited for consistency. For example, part 1, about the existence of the gods, also talks about the nature of god as fiery soul of the world, which should go in Part 2 under the qualities of the gods. Part 3, that the Gods govern the world, begins by proving the existence of the gods, repeating ideas that Part 1 already developed in detail. .

Part 5, a section about divination, is tacked onto the end of the discourse, though it was not mentioned in the plan that Balbus laid out at the beginning of the discourse. It seems that Cicero changed his plans while writing this discourse and decided to add this fifth section, but he did not go back and edit the plan at the beginning to make it consistent with what he ended up writing.

The styles of the sections are also different. Part 1 is a

digest of Stoic opinions that is repetitive, making it look like it is a collection of opinions from various Stoics. Part 2 is clearly a unified whole that systematically discusses the three types of divine beings. Part 3 is a unified and well reasoned philosophical treatise. Part 4 is unified but it is more polemical than philosophical, and it includes self-contradictions. Part 5 is unified but seems improvised.

Here, we present them as five separate works. If you read through them one after another, you will find that they are interesting to read as separate documents but are repetitive and confusing if they are all read as a single document.

Rackham says that he believes this discourse is based on a work of Posidonius, for three reasons. Posidonius (unlike most Stoics) included historical and literary illustrations of his ideas in his works, he was interested in science, and he admired Plato and Aristotle.[26] We have seen that Cicero inserts historical and literary illustrations in his source documents in many places, so this reason is not valid.

After we have broken up the discourse into five source works, we can see that the interest in science and the admiration of Aristotle is present in only one of them, Part 3, that the gods govern the world. The admiration of Plato is in Part 1, on the existence of the gods, which seems to be a collection of Stoic opinions from a variety of sources rather than a coherent treatise by a philosopher. Thus, Rackham gives us reasons to believe that Part 3 reproduces a work of Posidonius, not the entire discourse.

While reading the works, bear in mind that in Cicero's dialog, Lucilius Balbus represents the Stoic position, Velleius the Epicurean position, and Cotta the skeptical Academic position.

Cicero's Framing of the Five Works

i ".... For my part," rejoined Balbus, "I had rather listen to Cotta again, using the same eloquence that he employed

---

26 Cicero, *Nature of the Gods and Academics*, translated by H. Rackham (Harvard University Press, Loeb Classical Library, 1933-2000) p. xvii.

in abolishing false gods to present a picture of the true ones. A philosopher, a pontiff and a Cotta should possess not a shifting and unsettled conception of the immortal gods, like the Academics, but a firm and definite one like our school. ..."

"Have you forgotten," said Cotta, "what I said at the outset, that I find it more easy, especially on such subjects as these, to say what I don't think than what I do? Even if I had any clear view, I should still prefer to hear you speak in your turn, now that I have said so much myself."

"Well," replied Balbus, "I will yield to your wish; and I shall be as brief as I can, for indeed when the errors of Epicurus have been refuted, my argument is robbed of all occasion for prolixity. To take a general view, the topic of the immortal gods which you raise is divided by our school into four parts: first they prove that the gods exist; next they explain their nature; then they show that the world is governed by them; and lastly that they care for the fortunes of mankind. In our present discourse however let us take the first two of these heads; the third and fourth, being questions of greater magnitude, had better I think be put off to another time."

"No, no," cried Cotta, "we are at leisure now, and moreover the subjects which we are discussing might fitly claim precedence even of matters of business."

1: Stoic Proofs of the Existence of Gods
by unknown doxographers and Cicero
from *De Natura Deorum* II: ii-xvi

Introduction

It seems clear that this part of the discourse is a collection of Stoic doctrines rather than a unified whole. It includes summaries of ideas of Cleanthes, Chrysippus, Zeno, and ideas from other sources. These summaries are so brief that they seem to be by doxographers rather than being taken from the works of the philosophers themselves: for example, 300 words summarizing Cleanthes followed by 250 words summarizing Chrysippus.

Balbus initially says that the existence of the gods "seems not even to require arguing," but after going through a number of arguments, he reverses himself and says, "However, having begun to treat the subject in a different way from that which I proposed at the beginning (for I said that this part required no discussion, since the existence of god was manifest to everybody)," and then he goes on to give even more arguments for their existence. This inconsistency makes this part of the discourse sound like Cicero based it on a number of works.

Because Cicero compiled it from a number of sources that gave brief summaries of the philosophers' opinions, we attribute this work to Cicero and unknown doxographers.

All Agree that Gods Exist

ii "The first point," resumed Lucilius [Balbus], " For when we gaze upward to the sky and contemplate the heavenly bodies, what can be so obvious and so manifest as that there must exist some power possessing transcendent intelligence by whom these things are ruled … a deity omnipresent and omnipotent?

"If a man doubts this, I really cannot see why he should not also be capable of doubting the existence of the sun; how is the latter fact more evident than the former? Nothing but the presence in our minds of a firmly grasped concept of the deity could account for the stability and permanence of our belief in him, a belief which is only strengthened by the passage of the ages and grows more deeply rooted with each successive generation of mankind. In every other case we see that fictitious and unfounded opinions have dwindled away with lapse of time. Who believes that the Hippocentaur or the Chimaera ever existed? Where can you find an old wife senseless enough to be afraid of the monsters of the lower world that were once believed in? The years obliterate the inventions of the imagination, but confirm the judgments of nature.

"Hence both in our own nation and among all others reverence for the gods and respect for religion grow continually stronger and more profound.

…

iv "…. Hence the main issue is agreed among all men of all nations, inasmuch as all have engraved in their minds an innate belief that the gods exist.

v "As to their nature there are various opinions, but their existence nobody denies.

Cleanthes on Men's Ideas of the Gods

"Indeed our master Cleanthes gave four reasons to account for the formation in men's minds of their ideas of the gods. He put first the argument … arising from our foreknowledge of future events; second, the one drawn from the magnitude of the benefits which we derive from our temperate climate, from the earth's fertility, and from a vast abundance of other blessings; third, the awe inspired by lightning, storms, rain, snow, hail, floods, pestilences, earthquakes and occasionally subterranean rumblings, showers of stones and raindrops the color of blood, also landslips and chasms suddenly opening in the ground, also unnatural monstrosities human and animal, and also the appearance of meteoric lights and what are called by the Greeks 'comets,' and in our language 'long-haired stars,' such as recently during the Octavian War appeared as harbingers of dire disasters, ... And the fourth and most potent cause of the belief he said was the uniform motion and revolution of the heavens, and the varied groupings and ordered beauty of the sun, moon and stars, the very sight of which was in itself enough to prove that these things are not the mere effect of chance.

"When a man goes into a house, a wrestling-school or a public assembly and observes in all that goes on arrangement, regularity and system, he cannot possibly suppose that these things come about without a cause: he realizes that there is someone who presides and controls. Far more therefore with the vast movements and phases of the heavenly bodies, and these ordered processes of a multitude of enormous masses of matter, which throughout the countless ages of the infinite past have never in the smallest degree played false, is he compelled to infer that these mighty world-motions are regulated by some Mind.

Chrysippus on the Existence of the Gods

vi "Extremely acute of intellect as is Chrysippus, nevertheless his utterance here might well appear to have been learnt from the very lips of Nature, and not discovered by himself. 'If (he says) there be something in the world that man's mind and human reason, strength and power are incapable of producing, that which produces it must necessarily be superior to man; now the heavenly bodies and all those things that display a never-ending regularity cannot be created by man; therefore that which creates them is superior to man; yet what better name is there for this than 'god'? Indeed, if gods do not exist, what can there be in the universe superior to man? for he alone possesses reason, which is the most excellent thing that can exist; but for any human being in existence to think that there is nothing in the whole world superior to himself would be an insane piece of arrogance; therefore there is something superior to man; therefore God does exist.'

"Again, if you see a spacious and beautiful house, you could not be induced to believe, even though you could not see its master, that it was built by mice and weasels; if then you were to imagine that this elaborate universe, with all the variety and beauty of the heavenly bodies and the vast quantity and extent of sea and land, were your abode and not that of the gods, would you not be thought absolutely insane?

A Soul Pervades the World

"Again, do we not understand that everything in a higher position is of greater value, and that the lowest thing, and is enveloped by a layer of the densest kind of air? Hence for the same reason what we observe to be the case with certain districts and cities, I mean that their inhabitants are duller-witted than the average owing to the more compressed quality of the atmosphere, has also befallen the human race as a whole owing to its being located on the earth, that is, in the densest region of the world. Yet even man's intelligence must lead us to infer the existence of a mind in the universe, and that a mind of surpassing ability, and in fact divine. Otherwise, whence did man 'pick up' (as Socrates says in Xenophon) the intelligence that he possesses?

"If anyone asks the question, whence do we get the moisture and the heat diffused throughout the body, and the actual earthy substance of the flesh, and lastly the breath of life within us, it is manifest that we have derived the one from earth, the other from water, and the other from the air which we inhale in breathing.

vii "But where did we find, whence did we abstract, that

other part of us which surpasses all of these, I mean our reason, or, if you like to employ several terms to denote it, our intelligence, deliberation, thought, wisdom? Is the world to contain each of the other elements but not this one, the most precious of them all?

"Yet beyond question nothing exists among all things that is superior to the world, nothing that is more excellent or more beautiful; and not merely does nothing superior to it exist, but nothing superior can even be conceived. And if there be nothing superior to reason and wisdom, these faculties must necessarily be possessed by that being which we admit to be superior to all others.

"Again, consider the sympathetic agreement, interconnection and affinity of things: whom will this not compel to approve the truth of what I say? Would it be possible for the earth at one definite time to be gay with flowers and then in turn all bare and stark, or for the spontaneous transformation of so many things about us to signal the approach and the retirement of the sun at the summer and the winter solstices, or for the tides to flow and ebb in the seas and straits with the rising and setting of the moon, or for the different courses of the stars to be maintained by the one revolution of the entire sky? These processes and this musical harmony of all the parts of the world assuredly would not go on were they not maintained in unison by a single divine and all-pervading spirit.

Zeno's Syllogisms

"When one expounds these doctrines in a fuller and more flowing style, as I propose to do, it is easier for them to evade the captious objections of the Academy; but when they are reduced to brief syllogistic form, as was the practice of Zeno, they lie more open to criticism. A running river can almost or quite entirely escape pollution, whereas an enclosed pool is easily sullied; similarly a flowing stream of eloquence sweeps aside the censures of the critic, but a closely reasoned argument defends itself with difficult. The thoughts that we expound at length Zeno used to compress into this form:

viii " 'That which has the faculty of reason is superior to that which has not the faculty of reason; but nothing is superior to the world; therefore the world has the faculty of reason.' A similar argument can be used to prove that the world is wise, and happy, and eternal; for things possessed of each of these attributes are superior to things devoid of them, and nothing is superior to the world. From this it will follow that the world is god. Zeno also argued thus: 'Nothing devoid of sensation can have a part of itself that is sentient; but the world has parts that are sentient; therefore the world has parts that are sentient; therefore the world is not devoid of sensation.'

He also proceeds to press the argument more closely: 'Nothing,' he says, 'that is inanimate and irrational can give birth to an animate and rational being; but the world gives birth to animate and rational beings; therefore the world is animate and rational.'

Furthermore he proved his argument by means of one of his favorite comparisons, as follows: 'If flutes playing musical tunes grew on an olive-tree, surely you would not question that the olive-tree possessed some knowledge of the art of flute-playing; or if plane-trees bore well-tuned lutes, doubtless you would likewise infer that the plane-trees possessed the art of music; why then should we not judge the world to be animate and endowed with wisdom, when it produces animate and wise offspring?

Arguments from Natural Philosophy

ix "However, having begun to treat the subject in a different way from that which I proposed at the beginning (for I said that this part required no discussion, since the existence of god was manifest to everybody), in spite of this I should like to prove even this point by means of arguments drawn from Physics or Natural Philosophy. It is a law of Nature that all things capable of nurture and growth contain within them a supply of heat, without which their nurture and growth would not be possible; for everything of a hot, fiery nature supplies its own source of motion and activity; but that which is nourished and grows possesses a definite and uniform motion; and as long as this motion remains within us, so long sensation and life remain, whereas so soon as our heat is cooled and quenched we ourselves perish and are extinguished.

"This doctrine Cleanthes enforces by these further arguments, to show how great is the supply of heat in every living body: he states that there is no food so heavy that it is not digested in twenty-four hours; and even the residue of our food which nature rejects contains heat. Again, the veins and arteries never cease throbbing with a flame-like pulse, and frequent cases have been observed when the heart of an animal on being torn out of its body has continued to beat with a rapid motion resembling the flickering of fire. Every living thing therefore, whether animal or vegetable, owes its vitality to the heat contained within it. From this it must be inferred that this element of heat possesses in itself a vital force that pervades the whole world.

"We shall discern the truth of this more readily from a more detailed account of this all–permeating fiery element as a whole. All the parts of the world (I will however only specify the most important) are supported and sustained by heat. This can be perceived first of all in the element of earth. We see fire produced by striking or rubbing stones together; and when newly dug, 'the earth doth steam with warmth'; and also warm water is drawn from running springs, and this occurs most of all in the winter-time, because a great store of heat is confined in the caverns of the earth, which in winter is denser and therefore confines more closely the heat stored in the soil.

x "It would require a long discourse and a great many arguments to enable me to show that all the seeds that earth receives in her womb, and all the plants which she spontaneously generates and holds fixed by their roots in the ground, owe both their origin and growth to this warm temperature of the soil. That water also contains an admixture of heat is shown first of all by its liquid nature; water would neither be frozen into ice by cold nor congealed into snow and hoar-frost unless it could also become fluid when liquefied and thawed by the admixture of heat; this is why moisture both hardens when exposed to a north wind or a frost from some other quarter, and also in turn softens when warmed, and evaporates with heat. Also the sea when violently stirred by the wind becomes warm, so that it can readily be realized that this great body of fluid contains heat; for we must not suppose the warmth in question to be derived from some external source, but stirred up from the lowest depths of the sea by violent motion, just as happens to our bodies when they are restored to warmth by movement and exercise. Indeed the air itself, though by nature the coldest of the elements, is by no means entirely devoid of heat; indeed it contains even a considerable admixture of heat, for it is itself generated by exhalation from water, since air must be deemed to be a sort of vaporized water, and this vaporization is caused by the motion of the heat contained in the water. We may see an example of the same process when water is made to boil by placing fire beneath it. — There remains the fourth element: this is itself by nature glowing hot throughout and also imparts the warmth of health and life to all other substances.

"Hence from the fact that all the parts of the world are sustained by heat the inference follows that the world itself also owes its continued preservation for so long a time to the same or a similar substance, and all the more so because it must be understood that this hot and fiery principle is interfused with the whole of nature in such a way as to constitute the male and female generative principles, and so to be the necessary cause of both the birth and the growth of all living creatures, whether animals or those whose roots are planted in the earth.

xi "There is therefore an element that holds the whole world together and preserves it, and this an element possessed of sensation and reason; since every natural object that is not a homogeneous and simple substance but a complex and composite one must contain within it some ruling principle, for example in man the intelligence, in the lower animals something resembling intelligence that is the source of appetition. With trees and plants the ruling principle is believed to be located in the roots. I use the term 'ruling principle' as the equivalent of the Greek *hêgemonikon*, meaning that part of anything which must and ought to have supremacy in a thing of that sort. Thus it follows that the element which contains the ruling principle of the whole of nature must also be the most excellent of all things and the most deserving of authority and sovereignty over all things. Now we observe that the parts of the world (and nothing exists in all the world which is not a part of the whole world) possess sensation and reason. Therefore it follows that that part which contains the ruling principle of the world must necessarily possess sensation and reason, and these in a more intense and higher form. Hence it follows that the world possesses wisdom, and that the element which holds all things in its embrace is pre-eminently and perfectly rational, and therefore that the world is god, and all the forces of the world are held together by the divine nature.

"Moreover that glowing heat of the world is far purer and more brilliant and far more mobile, and therefore more stimulating to the senses, than this warmth of ours by which the things that we know are preserved and vitalized. As therefore man and the animals are possessed by this warmth and owe to this their motion and sensation, it is absurd to say that the world is devoid of sensation, considering that it is possessed by an intense heat that is stainless, free and purpose, and also penetrating and mobile in the extreme; especially as this intense world-heat does not derive its motion from the operation of some other force from outside, but is self-moved and spontaneous in its activity: for how can there be anything more powerful than the world, to impart motion and activity in the warmth by which the world is held together?

xii "For let us hear Plato, that divine philosopher, for so almost he is to be deemed. He holds that motion is of two sorts, one spontaneous, the other derived from without; and that that which moves of itself spontaneously is more divine than that which has motion imparted to it by some force not its own. The former kind of motion he deems to reside only in the soul, which he considers to be the only source and origin of motion. Hence, since all motion springs from the world-heat, and since that heat moves spontaneously and not by any impulse from something else, it follows that that heat is soul; which proves that the world is an animate being.

More Proofs that the World is a God

"Another proof that the world possesses intelligence is supplied by the fact that the world is unquestionably better than any of its elements; for even as there is no part of our body that is not of less value than we are ourselves, so the whole universe must needs be of higher worth than any portion of the universe; and if this be so, it follows that the world must be endowed with wisdom, for, if it were not, man, although a part of the world, being possessed of reason would necessarily be of higher worth than the world as a whole.

"Again, if we wish to proceed from the first rudimentary orders of being to the last and most perfect, we shall necessarily arrive in the end at deity. We notice the sustaining power of nature first in the members of the vegetable kingdom, towards which her bounty was limited to providing for their preservation by means of the faculties of nurture and growth. Upon the animals she bestowed sensation and motion, and an appetite or impulse to approach things wholesome and retire from things harmful. For man she amplified her gift by the addition of reason, whereby the appetites might be controlled, and alternately indulged and held in check.

xiii "But the fourth and highest grade is that of beings

born by nature good and wise, and endowed from the outset with the innate attributes of right reason and consistency; this must be held to be above the level of man: it is the attribute of god, that is, of the world, which must needs possess that perfect and absolute reason of which I spoke.

"Again, it is undeniable that every organic whole must have an ultimate ideal of perfection. As in vines or cattle we see that, unless obstructed by some force, nature progresses on a certain path of her own to her goal of full development, and as in painting, architecture and the other arts and crafts there is an ideal of perfect workmanship, even so and far more in the world of nature as a whole there must be a process towards completeness and perfection. The various limited modes of being may encounter many external obstacles to hinder their perfect realization, but there can be nothing that can frustrate nature as a whole, since she embraces and contains within herself all modes of being. Hence it follows that there must exist this fourth and highest grade, unassailable by any external force. Now this is the grade on which universal nature stands; and since she is of such a character as to be superior to all things and incapable of frustration by any, it follows of necessity that the world is an intelligent being, and indeed also a wise being.

"Again, what can be more illogical than to deny that the being which embraces all things must be the best of all things, or, admitting this, to deny that it must be, first, possessed of life, secondly, rational and intelligent, and lastly, endowed with wisdom? How else can it be the best of all things? If it resembles plants or even animals, so far from being highest, it must be reckoned lowest in the scale of being. If again it be capable of reason yet has not been wise from the beginning, the world must be in a worse condition than mankind; for a man can become wise, but if in all the eternity of past time the world has been foolish, obviously it will never attain wisdom; and so it will be inferior to man, which is absurd. Therefore the world must be deemed to have been wise from the beginning, and divine.

"In fact there is nothing else beside the world that has

nothing wanting, but is fully equipped and complete and perfect in all its details and parts.

xiv "For as Chrysippus cleverly puts it, just as a shield-case is made for the sake of a shield and a sheath for the sake of a sword, so everything else except the world was created for the sake of some other thing; thus the corn and fruits produced by the earth were created for the sake of animals, and animals for the sake of man: for example the horse for riding, the ox for ploughing, the dog for hunting and keeping guard; man himself however came into existence for the purpose of contemplating and imitating the world; he is by no means perfect, but he is 'a small fragment of that which is perfect.' The world on the contrary, since it embraces all things and since nothing exists which is not within it, is entirely perfect; how then can it fail to possess that which is the best? but there is nothing better than intelligence and reason; the world therefore cannot fail to possess them. Chrysippus therefore also well shows by the aid of illustrations that in the perfect and mature specimen of its kind everything is better than in the imperfect, for instance in a horse than in a foal, in a dog than in a puppy, in a man than in a boy; and that similarly a perfect and complete being is bound to possess that which is the best thing in all the world; but no being is more perfect than the world, and nothing is better than virtue; therefore virtue is an essential attribute of the world. Again, man's nature is not perfect, yet virtue may be realized in man; how much more readily then in the world! therefore the world possesses virtue. Therefore it is wise, and consequently divine.

The Stars as Gods

xv "Having thus perceived the divinity of the world, we must also assign the same divinity to the stars, which are formed from the most mobile and the purest part of the aether, and are not compounded of any other element besides; they are of a fiery heat and translucent throughout.

Hence they too have the fullest right to be pronounced to be living beings endowed with sensation and intelligence.

"That the stars consist entirely of fire Cleanthes holds to be established by the evidence of two of the senses, those of touch and sight. For the radiance of the sun is more brilliant than that of any fire, inasmuch as it casts its light so far and wide over the boundless universe; and the contact of its rays is so powerful that it not merely warms but often actually burns, neither of which things could it do if it were not made of fire.

"'Therefore,' Cleanthes proceeds, 'since the sun is made of fire, and is nourished by the vapors exhaled from the ocean because no fire could continue to exist without sustenance of some sort, it follows that it resembles either that fire which we employ in ordinary life or that which is contained in the bodies of living creatures. Now our ordinary fire that serves the needs of daily life is a destructive agency, consuming everything, and also wherever it spreads it routs and scatters everything. On the other hand the fire of the body is the glow of life and health; it is the universal preservative, giving nourishment, fostering growth, sustaining, bestowing sensation.'

"He therefore maintains that there can be no doubt which of the two kinds of fire the sun resembles, for the sun also causes all things to flourish and to bring forth increase each after its kind. Hence since the sun resembles those fires which are contained in the bodies of living creatures, the sun also must be alive; and so too the other heavenly bodies, since they have their origin in the fiery heat of heaven that is entitled the aether or sky. Since therefore some living creatures are born on the earth, others in the water and others in the air, it is absurd, so Aristotle holds, to suppose that no living animal is born in that element which is most adapted for the generation of living things. But the stars occupy the region of aether, and as this has a very rarefied substance and is always in lively motion, it follows that the animal born in this region has the keenest senses and the swiftest power of movement; hence since the stars come into existence in the aether, it is reasonable to suppose that they possess sensation and intelligence. And from this it follows that the stars are to be reckoned as gods.

xvi "For it may be observed that the inhabitants of those countries in which the air is pure and rarefied have keener wits and greater powers of understanding than persons who live in a dense and heavy climate; moreover the substance employed as food is also believed to have some influence on mental acuteness; it is therefore likely that the stars possess surpassing intelligence, since they inhabit the ethereal region of the world and also are nourished by the moist vapors of sea and earth, rarefied in their passage through the wide intervening space. Again, the consciousness and intelligence of the stars is most clearly evinced by their order and regularity; for regular and rhythmical motion is impossible without design, which contains no trace of casual or accidental variation; now the order and eternal regularity of the constellations indicates neither a process of nature, for it is highly rational, nor chance, for chance loves variation and abhors regularity; it follows therefore that the stars move of their own free-will and because of their intelligence and divinity.

Aristotle is also to be commended for his view that the motion of all living bodies is due to one of three causes, nature, force, or will; now the sun and moon and all the stars are in motion, and bodies moved by nature travel either downwards owing to their weight or upwards owing to their lightness; but neither (he argued) is the case with the heavenly bodies, because their motion is revolution in a circle; nor yet can it be said that some stronger force compels the heavenly bodies to travel in a manner contrary to their nature, for what stronger force can there be? it remains therefore that the motion of the heavenly bodies is voluntary.

Conclusion to the Work

"Anyone who sees this truth would show not only ignorance but wickedness if he denied the existence of the gods. Nor indeed does it make much difference whether he denies their existence or deprives them entirely of providential care and of activity; since to my mind an entirely inactive being cannot be said to exist at all. Therefore the existence of the gods is so manifest that I can scarcely deem one who denies it to be of sound mind.

2: On the Nature of the Gods
by an unknown Stoic Philosopher
from *De Natura Deorum* II: xvii-xxviii

Introduction

This selection provides an interesting perspective on medieval and Christian reasoning about the nature of God, because it uses some similar arguments but comes to totally different conclusions.

For example, the Christian St. Anselm argued that God is that than which there is nothing more perfect, and perfection must include existence. This work uses similar arguments to prove that the entire universe must be god, because nothing can be more excellent than the entire universe, and to prove that god must be a sphere (as the Stoics believed the universe was) because the sphere is the most perfect shape.

Christians argue that the motions of the heavenly bodies are so regular that they must be guided by a rational intelligence. This work uses a similar argument to claim that the heavenly bodies themselves must be gods.

In addition to the universe as a whole and the stars, this work preserves the traditional Greek gods by allegorizing them as representatives of abstractions or of natural phenomena, using imaginative etymologies for the gods' names. This allegorizing was common among Stoics, but it seems to contradict the earlier arguments used to prove that the universe is god, such as the argument that god must be a sphere

This section of the discourse clearly is a unified whole, but we have no way of knowing its author.

Cicero's Framing of this Work

xvii "It remains for us to consider the qualities of the divine nature; and on this subject nothing is more difficult than to divert the eye of the mind from following the practice of bodily sight. This difficulty has caused both uneducated people generally and those philosophers who resemble the uneducated to be unable to conceive of the immortal gods without setting before themselves the form of men: a shallow mode of thought which Cotta has exposed and which therefore calls for no discussion from me. But assuming that we have a definite and preconceived idea of a deity as, first, a living being, and secondly, a being unsurpassed in excellence by anything else in the whole of nature, I can see nothing that satisfies this preconception or idea of ours more fully than, first, the judgment that this world, which must necessarily be the most excellent of all things, is itself a living being and a god.

The Universe is God

"Let Epicurus jest at this notion as he will—and he is a person who jokes with difficulty, and has but the slightest smack of his native Attic wit,—let him protest his inability to conceive of god as a round and rotating body. Nevertheless he will never dislodge me from one belief which even he himself accepts: he holds that gods exist, on the ground that there must necessarily be some mode of being of outstanding and supreme excellence; now clearly nothing can be more excellent than the world. Nor can it be doubted that a living being endowed with sensation, reason and intelligence must excel a being devoid of those attributes; hence it follows that the world is a living being and possesses sensation, intelligence and reason; and this argument leads to the conclusion that the world is god.

"But these points will appear more readily a little later merely from a consideration of the creatures that the world produces.

xviii "In the meantime, pray, Velleius, do not parade

your school's utter ignorance of science. You say that you think a cone, a cylinder and a pyramid more beautiful than a sphere. Why, even in matters of taste you Epicureans have a criterion of your own! However, assuming that the figures which you mention are more beautiful to the eye—though for my part I don't think them so, for what can be more beautiful than the figure that encircles and encloses in itself all other figures, and that can possess no roughness or point of collision on its defense, no indentation of the concavity, no protuberance or depression? There are two forms that excel all others, among solid bodies the globe (for so we may translate the Greek *sphaera*), and among plane figures the round or circle, the Greek *kyklos*; well then, these two forms alone possess the property of absolute uniformity in all their parts and of having every point on the circumference equidistant from the centre; and nothing can be more compact than that.

The Heavenly Bodies are Gods

"Still, if you Epicureans cannot see this, as you have never meddled with that learned dust,[27] could you not have grasped even so much of natural philosophy as to understand that the uniform motion and regular disposition of the heavenly bodies could not have been maintained with any other shape? Hence nothing could be more unscientific than your favorite assertion, that it is not certain that our world itself is round, since it may possibly have some other form, and there are countless numbers of worlds, all of different shapes. Had but Epicurus learnt that twice two are four he certainly would not talk like that; but while making his palate the test of the chief good, he forgets to lift up his eyes to what Ennius calls 'the palate of the sky.'

xix "For there are two kinds of heavenly bodies, some that travel from east to west in unchanging paths, without ever making the slightest deviation in their course, while the others perform two unbroken revolutions in the same

27 The ancients drew diagrams for geometrical demonstrations in dust.

paths and courses. Now both of these facts indicate at once the rotatory motion of the firmament, which is only possible with a spherical shape, and the circular revolutions of the heavenly bodies.

"Take first of all the sun, which is the chief of the celestial bodies. Its motion is such that it first fills the countries of the earth with a flood of light, and then leaves them in darkness now on one side and now on the other; for night is caused merely by the shadow of the earth, which intercepts the light of the sun. Its daily and nightly paths have the same regularity. Also the sun by at one time slightly approaching and at another time slightly receding causes a moderate variation of temperature. For the passage of about 365¼ diurnal revolutions of the sun completes the circuit of a year; and by bending its course now towards the north and now towards the south the sun causes summers and winters and the two seasons of which one follows the waning of winter and the other that of summer. Thus from the changes of the four seasons are derived the origins and causes of all those creatures which come into existence on land and in the sea.

"Again the moon in her monthly paths overtakes the yearly course of the sun; and her light wanes to its minimum when she approaches nearest to the sun, and waxes to its maximum each time that she recedes farthest from him. And not only is her shape and outline altered by her alternate waxing and waning or returning to her starting-point, but also her position in the sky, which at one time is in the north and another in the south. The moon's course also has a sort of winter and summer solstice; and she emits many streams of influence, which supply animal creatures with nourishment and stimulate their growth and which cause plants to flourish and attain maturity.

xx "Most marvelous are the motions of the five stars, falsely called planets or wandering stars — for a thing cannot be said to wander if it preserves for all eternity fixed and regular motions, forward, backward and in other directions. And this regularity is all the more marvelous in the case of the stars we speak of, because at one time they are hidden and at another they are uncovered again; now they approach, now retire; now precede, now follow; now move faster, now slower, now do not move at all but remain for a time stationary. On the diverse moons of the planets the mathematicians have based what they call the Great Year, which is completed when the sun, moon and five planets having all finished their courses have returned to the same positions relative to one another.

"The length of this period is hotly debated, but it must necessarily be a fixed and definite time. The planet called Saturn, the Greek name of which is *Phaenon* (the shiner), which is the farthest away from the earth, completes its orbit in about thirty years, in the course of which period it passes through a number of remarkable phases, at one time accelerating and at another time retarding its velocity, now disappearing in the evening, then reappearing in the morning, yet without varying in the least degree throughout all the ages of eternity, but always doing the same things at the same times. Below this and nearer to the earth moves the star of Jupiter, called *Phaëthon* (the blazing star), which completes the same circuit of the twelve signs of the zodiac in twelve years, and makes the same variations during its course as the star of Saturn. The orbit next below is that of *Pyroeis* (the fiery), which is called the star of Mars, and this covers the same orbit as the two planets above it in twenty-four months all but (I think) six days. Below this in turn is the star of Mercury, called by the Greeks *Stilbōn* (the gleaming), which completes the circuit of the zodiac in about the period of a year, and is never distant from the sun more than the space of a single sign, though it sometimes precedes the sun and sometimes follows it. Lowest of the five planets and nearest to the earth is the star of Venus, called in Greek *Phosphoros* (the light-bringer) and in Latin *Lucifer* when it precedes the sun, but when it follows it *Hesperos*; this planet completes its orbit in a year, traversing the sun with a sausage movement as do the planets above it, and never distant more than the space of two signs from the sun, though sometimes in front of it and sometimes behind it.

xxi "This regularity therefore in the stars, this exact punctuality throughout all eternity notwithstanding the great variety of their courses, is to me incomprehensible without rational intelligence and purpose. And if we observe these attributes in the planets, we cannot fail to enroll even them among the number of the gods.

"Moreover the so-called fixed stars also indicate the same intelligence and wisdom. Their revolutions recur daily with exact regularity. It is not the case that they are carried along by the aether or that their courses are fixed in the firmament, as most people ignorant of natural philosophy aver; for the aether is not of such a nature as to hold the stars and cause them to revolve by its own force, since being rare and translucent and of uniform diffused heat, the aether does not appear to be well adapted to contain the stars. Therefore the fixed stars have a sphere of their own, separate from and not attached to the aether. Now the continual and unceasing revolutions of these stars, marvelously and incredibly regular as they are, clearly show that these are endowed with divine power and intelligence; so that anyone who cannot perceive that they themselves possess divinity would seem to be incapable of understanding anything at all.

"In the heavens therefore there is nothing of chance or hazard, no error, no frustration, but absolute order, accuracy, calculation and regularity. Whatever lacks these qualities, whatever is false and spurious and full of error, belongs to the region between the earth and the moon (the last of the heavenly bodies), and to the surface of the earth. Anyone therefore who thinks that the marvelous order and incredible regularity of the heavenly bodies, which is the sole source of preservation and safety for all things, is not rational, himself cannot be deemed a rational thing.

Nature as Craftsman

"I therefore believe that I shall not be wrong if in discussing this subject I take my first principle from the prince of seekers after truth, Zeno himself.

xxii Now Zeno gives this definition of nature: 'nature (he

says) is a craftsmanlike fire, proceeding methodically to the work of generation.' For he holds that the special function of an art or craft is to create and generate, and that what in the processes of our arts is done by the hand is done with far more skilful craftsmanship by nature, that is, as I said, by that 'craftsmanlike' fire which is the teacher of the other arts.

And on this theory, while each department of nature is 'craftsmanlike,' in the sense of having a method or path marked out for it to follow, the nature of the world itself, which encloses and contains all things in its embrace, is styled by Zeno not merely 'craftsmanlike' but actually 'a craftsman,' whose foresight plans out the work to serve its use and purpose in every detail. And as the other natural substances are generated, reared and sustained each by its own seeds, so the world-nature experiences all those motions of the will, those impulses of conation and desire, that the Greeks call *hormae*, and follows these up with the appropriate actions in the same way as do we ourselves, who experience emotions and sensations.

Such being the nature of the world-mind, it can therefore correctly be designated as prudence or providence (for in Greek it is termed *pronoia*); and this providence is chiefly directed and concentrated upon three objects, namely to secure for the world, first, the structure best fitted for survival; next, absolute completeness; but chiefly, consummate beauty and embellishment of every kind.

Other Deities Are Allegories

xxiii "We have discussed the world as a whole, and we have also discussed the heavenly bodies; so that there now stands fairly well revealed to our view a vast company of gods who are neither idle nor yet perform their activities with irksome and laborious toil. For they have no framework of veins and sinews and bones; nor do they consume such kinds of food and drink as to make them contract too sharp or too sluggish a condition of the humors; nor are their bodies such as to make them fear falls or blows or apprehend disease from exhaustion of their members — dangers which led Epicurus to invent his unsubstantial, do-nothing gods. On the contrary, they are endowed with supreme beauty of form, they are situated in the purest region of the sky, and they so control their motions and courses as to seem to be conspiring together to preserve and to protect the universe.

"Many other divinities however have with good reason been recognized and named both by the wisest men of Greece and by our ancestors from the great benefits that they bestow. For it was thought that whatever confers great utility on the human race must be due to the operation of divine benevolence towards men. Thus sometimes a thing sprung from a god was called by the name of the god himself; as when we speak of corn as Ceres …. In other cases some exceptionally potent force is itself designated by a title of convey, for example Faith and Mind…. Again, there are the temples of Wealth, Safety, Concord, Liberty and Victory, all of which things, being so powerful as necessarily to imply divine governance, were themselves designated as gods. In the same class the names of Desire, Pleasure and Venus Lubentina have been deified — things vicious and unnatural (although Velleius thinks otherwise), yet the urge of these vices often overpowers natural instinct. Those gods therefore who were the authors of various benefits owned their deification to the value of the benefits which they bestowed, and indeed the names that I just now enumerated express the various powers of the gods that bear them.

xxiv "Human experience moreover and general custom have made it a practice to confer the deification of renown and gratitude upon of distinguished benefactors. This is the origin of Hercules, of Castor and Pollux, of Aesculapius, and also of Liber (I mean Liber the son of Semele …) — and this is also the origin of Romulus, who is believed to be the same as Quirinus. And these benefactors were duly deemed divine, as being both supremely good and immortal, because their souls survived and enjoyed eternal life.

"Another theory also, and that a scientific one, has been

the source of a number of deities, who clad in human form have furnished the poets legends and have filled man's life with superstitions of all sorts. This subject was handled by Zeno and was later explained more fully by Cleanthes and Chrysippus. For example, an ancient belief prevailed throughout Greece that Caelus[28] was mutilated by his son Saturn, and Saturn himself thrown into bondage by his son Jove: now these immoral fables enshrined a decidedly clever scientific theory. Their meaning was that the highest element of celestial ether or fire, which by itself generates all things, is devoid of that bodily part which requires union with another for the work of procreation.

xxv "By Saturn again they denoted that being who maintains the course and revolution of seasons and periods of time, et deity actually so designated in Greek, for Saturn's Greek name is *Kronos*, which is the same as *chronos*, a space of time. The Latin designation 'Saturn' on the other hand is due to the fact that he is 'saturated' or 'satiated with years' (*anni*); the fable is that he was in the habit of devouring his sons—meaning that Time devours the ages and gorges himself insatiably with the years that are past. Saturn was bound by Jove in order that Time's courses might not be unlimited, and that Jove might fetter him by the bonds of the stars.

"But Jupiter himself—the name means 'the helping father,' whom with a change of inflexion we style Jove, from *iuvare* 'to help'; the poets call him 'father of gods and men,' and our ancestors entitled him 'best and greatest,' putting the title 'best,' that is most beneficent, before that of 'greatest,' because universal beneficence is gate their, or at least more lovable, than the possession of great wealth.... It is he also whom our augurs mean by their formula 'should Jove lighten and thunder,' meaning 'should the sky lighten and thunder.' ...

xxvi "The air, lying between the sea and sky, is according to the Stoic theory deified under the name belonging to Juno,

28 Sky, Latin translation of Ouranos (Uranus), as Saturn is the translation of Kronos and Jove of Zeus.

sister and wife of Jove, because it resembles and is closely connected with the aether; they made it female and assigned it to Juno because of its extreme softness. (The name of Juno however I believe to be derived from *iuvare* 'to help').

"There remained water and earth, to complete the fabled partition of the three kingdoms. Accordingly the second kingdom, the entire realm of the sea, was assigned to Neptune, Jove's brother as they hold; his name is derived from *nare* 'to swim,' with a slight alteration of the earlier letters and with the suffix seen in Portunus (the harbor god), derived from *portus* 'a harbor.' The entire bulk and substance of the earth was dedicated to father Dis (that is, *Dives*, 'the rich,' and so in Greek *Plouton*), because all things fall back into the earth and also arise from the earth. He is said to have married Proserpina (really a Greek name, for she is the same as the goddess called Persephone in Greek) — they think that she represents the seed of corn, and fable that she was hidden away, and sought for by her mother. The mother is Ceres, a corruption of 'Geres,' from *gero*, because she bears the crops; the same accidental change of the first letter is also seen in her Greek name *Dêmêtêr*, a corruption of *gê mêtêr* ('mother earth').

"Mavors[29] again is from *magna vertere*, 'the overturner of the great,' while Minerva is either 'she who minishes' or 'she who is minatory.'

xxvii "Also, as the beginning and the end are the most important parts of all affairs, they held that Janus is the leader in a sacrifice, the name being derived from *ire* ('to go'), hence the names *jani* for archways and *januae* for the front doors of secular buildings. Again, the name Vesta comes from the Greeks, for she is the goddess whom they call Hestia. Her power extends over altars and hearths, and therefore all prayers and all sacrifices end with this goddess, because she is the guardian of the innermost things. Closely related to this function are the Penates or household gods, a name derived either from *penus*, which means a store of human food of any kind, or from the fact that they reside

29 An alternative name for Mars.

penitus, in the recesses of the house, owing to which they are also called *penetrales* by the poets.

"The name Apollo again is Greek; they say that he is the sun,29 and Diana they identify with the moon; the word *sol* being from *solus*, either because the sun 'alone' of all the heavenly bodies is of that magnitude, or because when the sun rises all the stars are dimmed and it 'alone' is visible; while the name Luna is derived from *lucere* 'to shine'; for it is the same word as Lucina, and therefore in our country Juno Lucina is invoked in childbirth, as is Diana in her manifestation as Lucifera (the light-bringer) among the Greeks. She is also called Diana Omnivaga (wide-wandering), not from her hunting, but because she is counted one of the seven planets or 'wanderers' (*vagari*). She was called Diana because she made a sort of day in the night-time. She is invoked to assist at birth of children, because the period of gestation is either occasionally seven, or more usually nine, lunar revolutions, and these are called *menses* (months), because they cover measured (*mensa*) spaces. Timaeus in his history with his usual aptness adds to his account of the burning of the temple of Diana of Ephesus on the night on which Alexander was born the remark that this need cause no surprise, since Diana was away from home, wishing to be present when Olympias was brought to bed.

Venus was so named by our countrymen as the goddess who 'comes' (*venire*) to all things; her name is not derived from the word *venustas* (beauty) but rather *venustas* from it.

xxviii "Do you see therefore how from a true and valuable philosophy of nature has been evolved this imaginary and fanciful pantheon? The perversion has been a fruitful source of false beliefs, crazy errors and superstitions hardly above the level of old wives' tales. We know what the gods look like and how old they are, their dress and their equipment, and also their genealogies, marriages and relationships, and all about them is distorted into the likeness of human frailty. They are actually represented as liable to passions and emotions — we hear of their being in love, sorrowful, angry; according to the myths they even engage in wars and battles, and that not only when as in Homer two armies and contending and the gods take sides and intervene on their behalf, but they actually fought wars of their own, for instance with the Titans and with the Giants. These stories and these beliefs are utterly foolish; they are stuffed with nonsense and absurdity of all sorts. But though repudiating these myths with contempt, we shall nevertheless be able to understand the personality and the nature of the divinities pervading the substance of the several elements, Ceres permeating earth, Neptune the sea, and so on; and it is our duty to revere and worship these gods under the names which custom has bestowed upon them.

Conclusion to the Work

"But the best and also the purest, holiest and most pious way of worshipping the gods is ever to venerate them with purity, sincerity and innocence both of thought and of speech.

"For religion has been distinguished from superstition not only by philosophers but by our ancestors. Persons who spent whole days in prayer and sacrifice to ensure that their children should outlive them were termed 'superstitious' (from *superstes*, a survivor), and the word later acquired a wider application. Those on the other hand who carefully reviewed and so to speak retraced all the lore of ritual were called 'religious' from *relegere* (to retrace or re-read), like 'elegant' from *eligere* (to select), 'diligent' from *diligere* (to care for), 'intelligent' from *intellegere* (to understand); for all these words contain the same sense of 'picking out' (*legere*) that is present in 'religious.' Hence 'superstitious' and 'religious' came to be terms of censure and approval respectively.

"I think that I have said enough to prove the existence of the gods and their nature."

3: The Gods Govern the World
probably by Posidonius
from *De Natura Deorum* II: xxix-xlvi

Introduction

This section is clearly a unified work. It begins by saying it will include three topics, and then it systematically discusses those three topics.

This work must have been written after the time of Panaetius, who rejected the traditional Stoic belief that the universe is destroyed in periodic conflagrations in favor of Aristotle's belief that the universe has existed forever, since it says "our school believe, though it used to be said that Panaetius questioned the doctrine, there will ultimately occur a conflagration of the whole...."[30]

As we saw in the introduction to the five works, Rackham gives us good reason to believe that this discourse is based on a work of Panaetius' successor, Posidonius, who was interested in science and admired Aristotle.[31] This work quotes Aristotle, saying that his statement is "brilliant," and includes a long discussion of astronomy that mentions the orrery of Posidonius.

Rakham also says that Posidonius includes literary and historical illustrations in his work, but we leave these out here, because they might also have been added by Cicero and because leaving them out makes this work more readable for students of philosophy.

The speaker begins by outlining the three topics of this

30 *De Natura Deorum* II: xlvi.

31 Cicero, *Nature of the Gods and Academics*, translated by H. Rackham (Harvard University Press, Loeb Classical Library, 1933-2000) p. xvii.

work. The first proves that the gods exist, so it follows that the world is governed by their wisdom. The second proves that all things are directed by sentient nature in the most beautiful manner, so it follows that the universe was generated from living first causes. The third topic is the argument from the wonder that we feel at the marvel of creation, celestial and terrestrial.

Notice that all of these points are also discussed in other parts of Balbus' discourse. For example, the existence of gods was discussed very thoroughly in its first section, and this section repeats some of its arguments. This repetition is clear evidence that Cicero created Balbus' discourse from a patchwork of different sources. He occasionally adds text trying to unify them, such as the final paragraph of the section the we named "Existence of Gods."

Cicero's Framing of this Work

xix "Next I have to show that the world is governed by divine providence. This is of course a vast topic; the doctrine is hotly contested by your school, Cotta [the skeptical Academy], and it is they no doubt that are my chief adversaries here. As for you and your friends, Velleius [the Epicureans], you scarcely understand the vocabulary of the subject; for you only read your own writings, and are so enamored of them that you pass judgment against all the other schools without giving them a hearing. For instance, you yourself told us yesterday that the Stoics present *Pronoia* or providence in the guise of an old hag of a fortune-teller; this was due to your mistaken notion that they imagine providence as a kind of special deity who rules and governs the universe. But as a matter of fact 'providence' is an elliptical expression; when one says 'the Athenian state is ruled by the council,' the words 'of the Areopagus' are omitted: so when we speak of the world as governed by providence, you must understand the words 'of the gods' and conceive that the full and complete statement would be 'the world is governed by the providence of the gods.' So do not you and your friends waste your wit on making fun of us, — your tribe is none too well off for that commodity. ...

xxx "I therefore declare that the world and all its parts were set in order at the beginning and have been governed for all time by divine providence: a thesis which our school usually divides into three sections. The first is based on the argument proving that the gods exist; if this be granted, it must be admitted that the world is governed by their wisdom. The second proves that all things are under the sway of sentient nature, and that by it the universe is carried on in the most beautiful manner; and this proved, it follows that the universe was generated from living first causes. The third topic is the argument from the wonder that we feel at the marvel of creation, celestial and terrestrial.

Existence of Gods

"In the first place therefore one must either deny the existence of the gods, which in a manner is done by Democritus when he represents them as 'apparitions' and by Epicurus with his 'images'; or anybody who admits that the gods exist must allow them activity, and activity of the most distinguished sort; now nothing can be more distinguished than the government of the world; therefore the world is governed by the wisdom of the gods. If this is not so, there must clearly be something better and more powerful than god, be it what it may, whether inanimate nature or necessity speeding on with mighty force to create the supremely beautiful objects that we see; in that case the nature of the gods is not superior to all else in power, inasmuch as it is subject to a necessity or nature that rules the sky, sea and land. But as a matter of fact nothing exists that is superior to god; it follows therefore that the world is ruled by him; therefore god is not obedient or subject to any form of nature, and therefore he himself rules all nature.

"In fact if we concede divine intelligence, we concede also divine providence, and providence exercised in things of the highest moment. Are then the gods ignorant what things are of the highest moment and how these are to be directed and upheld, or do they lack the strength to undertake and to perform duties so vast? But ignorance is foreign the time of divine nature, and weakness, with a consequent incapacity to perform one's office, in no way suits with the divine majesty. This proves our thesis that the world is governed by divine providence.

xxxi "And yet from the fact of the gods' existence (assuming that they exist, as they certainly do) it necessarily follows that they are animate beings, and not only animate but possessed of reason and united together in a sort of social community or fellowship, ruling the one world as a united commonwealth or state. It follows that they possess the same faculty of reason as the human race, and that both have the same apprehension of truth and the same law enjoining what is right and rejecting what is wrong. Hence we see that wisdom and intelligence also have been derived by men from the gods; and this explains why it was the practice of our ancestors to deify Mind, Faith, virtue and Concord, and to set up temples to them at the public charge, and how can we consistently deny that they exist with the gods, when we worship their majestic and holy images? And if mankind possesses intelligence, faith, virtue and concord, whence can these things have flowed down upon the earth if not from the powers above? Also since we possess wisdom, reason and prudence, the gods must needs possess them too in greater perfection, and not possess them merely but also exercise them upon matters of the greatest magnitude and value; but nothing is of greater magnitude and value than the universe; it follows therefore that the universe is governed by the wisdom and providence of the gods.

"Finally, since we have conclusively proved the divinity of those beings whose glorious might and shining aspect we behold, I mean the sun and moon and the planets and fixed stars, and the sky and the world itself, and all that mighty multitude of objects contained in all the world which are of great service and benefit to the human race, the conclusion is that all things are ruled by divine intelligence and wisdom. So much for the first division of my subject.

Sentient Nature Rules Things Excellently

xxxii "Next I have to show that all things are under the sway of nature and are carried on by her in the most excellent manner.

"But first I must briefly explain the meaning of the term 'nature' itself, to make our doctrine more easily intelligible. Some persons define nature as a non-rational force that causes necessary motions in material bodies; others as a rational and ordered force, proceeding by method and plainly displaying the means that she takes to produce each result and the end at which she aims, and possessed of a skill that no handiwork of artist or craftsman can rival or reproduce. For a seed, they point out, has such potency that, tiny though it is in size, nevertheless if it falls into some substance that conceives and enfolds it, and obtains suitable material to foster its nurture and growth, it fashions and produces the various creatures after their kinds, some designed merely to absorb nourishment through their roots, and others capable of motion, sensation, appetition and reproduction of their species. Some thinkers again denote by the term 'nature' the whole of existence—for example Epicurus, who divides the nature of all existing things into atoms, void, and the attributes of these. When we on the other hand speak of nature as the sustaining and governing principle of the world, we do not mean that the world is like a clod of earth or lump of stone or something else of that sort, which possesses only the natural principle of cohesion, but like a tree or an animal, displaying no haphazard structure, but order and a certain semblance of design.

xxxiii "But if the plants fixed and rooted in the earth owe their life and vigor to nature's art, surely the earth herself must be sustained by the same power, inasmuch as when impregnated with seeds she brings forth from her womb all things in profusion, nourishes their roots in her bosom and causes them to grow, and herself in turn is nourished by the upper and outer elements. Her exhalations moreover give nourishment to the air, the ether and all the heavenly bodies. Thus if earth is upheld and invigorated by nature, the same principle must hold good of the rest of the world, for plants are rooted in the earth, animals are sustained by breathing air, and the air itself is our partner in seeing, hearing and uttering sounds, since none of these actions can be performed without its aid; nay, it even moves as we move, for wherever we go or move our limbs, it seems as it were to give place and retire before us. And those things which travel towards the centre of the earth which is its lowest point, those which move from the centre upwards, and those which rotate in circles round the centre, constitute the one continuous nature of the world. Again the continuum of the world's nature is constituted by the cyclic transmutations of the four kinds of matter. For earth turns into water, water into air, air into aether, and then the process is reversed, and aether becomes air, air water, and water earth, the lowest of the four. Thus the parts of the world are held in union by the constant passage up and down, thenceforth, of these four elements of which all things are composed.

"And this world-structure must either be everlasting in this same form in which we see it or at all events extremely durable, and destined to endure for an almost immeasurably protracted period of time. Whichever alternative be true, the inference follows that the world is governed by nature. For consider the navigation of a fleet, the marshalling of an army, or (to return to instances from the processes of nature) the budding of a vine or of a tree, or even the shape and structure of the limbs of an animal—when do these ever evidence such a degree of skill in nature as the world itself? Either therefore there is nothing that is ruled by a sentient nature, or we must admit that the world is so ruled. Indeed, how is it possible that the universe, which contains within itself all the other natures and their seeds, should not itself be governed by nature? Thus if anyone declared that a man's teeth and the hair on his body are a natural growth but that the man himself to whom they belong is not a natural organism, he would fail to see that things which produce something from within them must have more perfect natures than the things which are produced from them.

xxxiv "But the sower and planter and begetter, so to speak, of all the things that nature governs, their trainer and nourisher, is the world; the world gives nutriment and sustenance to all its limbs as it were, or parts. But if the parts of the world are governed by nature, the world itself must needs be governed by nature.

"Now the government of the world contains nothing that could possibly be censured; given the existing elements, the best that could be produced from them has been produced. Let someone therefore prove that it could have been better. But no one will ever prove this, and anyone who essays to improve some detail will either make it worse or will be demanding an improvement impossible in the nature of things.

"But if the structure of the world in all its parts is such that it could not have been better whether in point of utility or beauty, let us consider whether this is the result of chance, or whether on the contrary the parts of the world are in such a condition that they could not possibly have cohered together if they were not controlled by intelligence and by divine providence. If then the products of nature are better than those of art, and if art produces nothing without reason, nature too cannot be deemed to be without reason. When you see a statue or a painting, you recognize the exercise of art; when you observe from a distance the course of a ship, you do not hesitate to assume that its motion is guided by reason and by art; when you look at a sun-dial or a water-clock, you infer that it tells the time by art and not by chance; how then can it be consistent to suppose that the world, which includes both the works of art in question, the craftsmen who made them, and everything else besides, can be devoid of purpose and of reason?

"Suppose a traveler to carry into Scythia or Britain the

orrery recently constructed by our friend Posidonius, which at each revolution reproduces the same motions of the sun, the moon and the five planets that take place in the heavens every twenty-four hours, would any single native doubt that this orrery was the work of a rational being? These thinkers however raise doubts about the world itself from which all things arise and have their being, and debate whether it is the produce of chance or necessity of some sort, or of divine reason and intelligence; they think more highly of the achievement of Archimedes in making a model of the revolutions of the firmament than of that of nature in creating them, although the perfection of the original shows a craftsmanship many times as great as does the counterfeit.

    ....

xxxvi "But as it is they appear to me to have no suspicion even of the marvels of the celestial and terrestrial creation. For in the first place the earth, which is situated in the centre of the world, is surrounded on all sides by this living and respirable substance named the air. 'Air' is a Greek word, but yet it has by this time been accepted in use by our race, and in fact passes current as Latin. The air in turn is embraced by the immeasurable aether, which consists of the most elevated portions of fire. The term 'aether' also we may borrow, and employ it like 'air' as a Latin word ....

"From aether then arise the innumerable fires of the heavenly bodies, chief of which is the sun, who illumines all things with most brilliant light, and is many times greater and vaster than the whole earth; and after him the other stars of unmeasured magnitudes. And these vast and numerous fires not merely do no harm to the earth and to terrestrial things, but are actually beneficial, though with the qualification that were their positions altered, the earth would inevitably be burnt up by such enormous volumes of heat when uncontrolled and untempered.

xxxvii "At this point must I not marvel that there should be anyone who can persuade himself that there are certain solid and indivisible particles of matter borne along by the force of gravity, and that the fortuitous collision of those particles produces this elaborate and beautiful world? I cannot understand why he who considers it possible for this to have occurred should not all think that, if a countless number of copies of the one-and-twenty letters of alphabet, made of gold or what you will, were thrown together into some receptacle and then shaken out on the ground, it would be possible that they should produce the *Annals* of Ennius, all ready for the reader. I doubt whether chance could possibly succeed in producing even a single verse! Yet according to the assertion of your friends, that out of particles of matter not endowed with heat, nor with any 'quality' (the Greek term *poiotes*), nor with sense, but colliding together at haphazard and by chance, the world has emerged complete, or rather a countless number of worlds are some of them being born and some perishing at every moment of time—yet if the clash of atoms can create a world, why can it not produce a colonnade, a temple, a house, a city, which are less and indeed much less difficult things to make? The fact is, they indulge in such random babbling about the world that for my part I cannot think that they have ever looked up at this marvelously beautiful sky—which is my next topic.

"So Aristotle says brilliantly: 'If there were beings who had always lived beneath the earth, in comfortable, well-lit dwellings, decorated with statues and pictures and furnished with all the luxuries enjoyed by persons thought to be supremely happy, and who though they had never come forth above the ground had learnt by report and by hearsay of the existence of certain deities or divine powers; and then if at some time the jaws of the earth were opened and they were able to escape from their hidden abode and to come forth into the regions which we inhabit; when they suddenly had sight of the earth and the seas and the sky, and came to know of the vast clouds and mighty winds, and beheld the sun, and realized not only its size and beauty but also its potency in causing the day by shedding light over all the sky, and, after night had darkened the earth, they then saw the whole sky spangled and adorned with stars, and the changing phases of the moon's light, now waxing and now waning, and the risings and settings of all these heavenly bodies and their courses fixed and changeless throughout all eternity,—when they saw these things, surely they would think that the gods exist and that these mighty marvels are their handiwork.'

xxxviii "Thus far Aristotle; let us for our part imagine a darkness as dense as that which is said to have once covered the neighboring districts on the occasion of an eruption of the volcano Etna, so that for two days no man could recognize his fellow, and when on the third day the sun shone upon them, they felt as if they had come to life again: well, suppose that after darkness had prevailed from the beginning of time, it similarly happened to ourselves suddenly to behold the light of day, what should we think of the splendor of the heavens? But daily recurrence and habit familiarize our indicates with the sight, and we feel no surprise or curiosity as to the reasons for things that we see always; just as if it were the novelty and not rather the importance of phenomena that ought to arouse us to inquire into their causes.

"Who would not deny the name of human being to a man who, on seeing the regular motions of the heaven and the fixed order of the stars and the accurate interconnection and interrelation of all things, can deny that these things possess any rational design, and can maintain that phenomena, the wisdom of whose ordering transcends the capacity of our wisdom to understand it, take place by chance? When we see something moved by machinery, like an orrery or clock or many other such things, we do not doubt that these contrivances are the work of reason; when therefore we behold the whole compass of the heaven moving with revolutions of marvelous velocity and executing with perfect regularity the annual changes of the seasons with absolute safety and security for all things, how can we doubt that all this is effected not merely by reason, but by a reason that is transcendent and divine?

The Argument from Wonder

"For we may now put aside elaborate argument and gaze as it were with our eyes upon the beauty of the creations of divine providence, as we declare them to be.

xxxix "And first let us behold the whole earth, situated in the centre of the world, a solid spherical mass gathered into a globe by the natural gravitation of all its parts, clothed with flowers and grass and trees and corn, forms of vegetation all of them incredibly numerous and inexhaustibly varied and diverse. Add to these cool fountains ever flowing, transparent streams and rivers, their banks clad in brightest verdure, deep vaulted caverns, craggy rocks, sheer mountain heights and plains of immeasurable extent; add also the hidden veins of gold and silver, and marble in unlimited quantity. Think of all the various species of animals, both tame and wild! think of the flights and songs of birds! of the pastures filled with cattle, and the teeming life of the woodlands!

Then why need I speak of the race of men? who are as it were the appointed tillers of the soil, and who suffer it not to become a savage haunt of monstrous beasts of prey nor a barren waste of thickets and brambles, and whose industry diversifies and adorns the lands and islands and coasts with houses and cities. Could we but behold these things with our eyes as we can picture them in our minds, no one taking in the whole earth at one view could doubt the divine reason.

"Then how great is the beauty of the sea! how glorious the aspect of its vast expanse! how many and how diverse its islands! how lovely the scenery of its coasts and shores! how numerous and how different the species of marine animals, some dwelling in the depths, some floating and swimming on the surface, some clinging in their own shells to the rocks! And the sea itself, yearning for the earth, sports against her shores in such a fashion that the two elements appear to be fused into one.

"Next the air bordering on the sea undergoes the alternates of day and night, and now rises upward melt down rarefied, now is condensed and compressed into clouds and gathering mixture enriches the earth with rain, now flows forth in currents thenceforth and produces winds. Likewise it causes the yearly variations of cold and heat, and it also both supports the flight of birds and inhaled by breathing nourishes and sustains the animal race.

xl "There remains the element that is most distant and highest removed from our abodes, the all-engirdling, all-confining circuit of the sky, also named the aether, the farthest coast and frontier of the world, wherein those fiery shapes most marvelously trace out their ordered courses. Of these the sun, which many times surpasses the earth in magnitude, revolves about her, and by his rising and setting causes day and night, and now approaching, then again retiring, twice each year makes returns in opposite directions from his farthest point, and in the period of those returns at one time causes the face of the earth as it were to contract with a gloomy frown, and at another restores her to gladness till she seems to smile in sympathy with the sky. Again the moon, which is, as the mathematicians prove, more than half the size of the earth, roams in the same courses as the sun, but at one time converging with the sun and at another diverging from it, both bestows upon the light that it has borrowed from the sun and itself undergoes divers changes of its light, and also at one time is in conjunction and hides the sun, darkening the light of its rays, at another itself comes into the shadow of the earth, being opposite to the sun, and owing to the interpose and interference of the earth is suddenly extinguished. And the so-called wandering stars (planets) travel in the same courses round the earth, and rise and set in the same way, with motions now accelerated, now retarded, and sometimes even ceasing altogether. Nothing can be more marvelous or more beautiful than this spectacle. Next comes the vast multitude of the fixed stars, grouped in constellations so clearly defined that they have received names derived from their resemblance to familiar objects."

...

[Here, another speaker interrupts and recites a long poem by Aratus about the wonders of nature]

xliv ".... Can any sane person believe that all this array of stars and this vast celestial adornment could have been created out of atoms rushing thenceforth fortuitously and at random? or could any other being devoid of intelligence and reason have created them? Not merely did their creation postulate intelligence, but it is impossible to understand their nature without intelligence of a high order.

xlv "But not only are these things marvelous, but nothing is more remarkable than the stability and coherence of the world, which is such that it is impossible even to imagine anything better adapted to endure. For all its parts in every direction gravitate with a uniform pressure towards the center. Moreover bodies conjoined maintain their union most permanently when they have some bond encompassing them to bind them together; and this function is fulfilled by that rational and intelligent substance which pervades the whole world as the efficient cause of all things and which draws and collects the outermost particles towards the centre.

"Hence if the world is round and therefore all its parts are held together by and with each other in universal equilibrium, the same must be the case with the earth, so that all its parts must converge towards the centre (which in a sphere is the lowest point) without anything to break the continuity and so threaten its vast complex of gravitational forces and masses with dissolution. And on the same principle the sea, although above the earth, nevertheless seeks the earth's centre and so is massed into a sphere uniform on all sides, and never floods its bounds and overflows. Its neighbor the air travels upward it is true in virtue of its lightness, but at the same time spreads horizontally in all directions; and thus while contiguous and conjoined with the sea it has a natural tendency to rise to the sky, and by receiving an admixture of the sky's tenuity and heat furnishes to living creatures the breath of life and health. The air is enfolded by the highest part of the sky, termed the ethereal part; this both retains its own tenuous warmth uncongealed by any admixture and unites with the outer surface of the air.

xlvi "In the aether the stars revolve in their courses; these maintain their spherical form by their own internal gravitation, and also sustain their motions by virtue of their very shape and conformation; for they are round, and this is the shape, as I believe I remarked before, that is least capable of receiving injury. But the stars are of a fiery substance, and for this reason they are nourished by the vapors of the earth, the sea and the waters, which are raised up by the sun out of the fields which it warms and out of the waters; and when nourished and renewed by these vapors the stars and the whole aether shed them back again, and then once more draw them up from the same source, with the loss of none of their matter, or only of an extremely small part which is consumed by the fire of the stars and the flame of the aether.

"As a consequence of this, so our school believe, though it used to be said that Panaetius questioned the doctrine, there will ultimately occur a conflagration of the whole world, because when the moisture has been used up neither can the earth be nourished nor will the air continue to flow, being unable to rise upward after it has drunk up all the water; thus nothing will remain but fire, by which, as a living being and a god, once again a new world may be created and the ordered universe be restored as before.

"I would not have you think that I dwell too long upon astronomy, and particularly upon the system of the stars called planets; these with the most diverse movements work in such mutual harmony that the uppermost, that of Saturn, has a cooling influence, the middle planet, that of Mars, imparts heat, the one between them, that of Jove, gives light and a moderate warmth, while two beneath Mars obey the sun, and the sun itself fills all the world with light, and also illuminates the moon, which is the source of conception and birth and of growth and maturity. If any man is not impressed by this co-ordination of things and this harmonious combination of nature to secure the preservation of the world, I know for certain that he has never given any consideration to these matters.

4: The Gods Care for Plants, Animals and Man

by an unknown Stoic polemicist
from *De Natura Deorum* II: xlvii-lxiv

Introduction

This section is clearly a unified work in praise of providence and nature.

It does not follow naturally from what came before. "That the Gods Govern the World" began by saying that it was divided into three parts, those three parts have been completed, and this section shifts to a new subject with its initial statement, "Here somebody will ask, for whose sake was all this vast system contrived?" This section mentions "wonder" a couple of times to connect it with the previous section about the argument from wonder, but this is presumably a transitional device that Cicero added: if it were a continuation of the argument from wonder in the previous work, the argument from wonder would be far, far longer than the other sections of that work.

The style is also different from the previous work, since it is more polemical than philosophical. The previous work does become polemical at times, particularly in its final part about the "argument from wonder," but this section gets so carried away with its polemic that it falls into self-contradictions. For example, it says that god has been good to man because "all the senses of man far excel those of the lower animals,"[32] but later it says that god has been good to man because we can use animals whose senses are sharper than ours: "we divert to our service the marvelously acute senses of elephants and the keen scent of hounds."[33]

Its praise of nature is sometimes obviously unrealistic: he says that god has provided food for all animals, but it ignores hunger and predation among animals. Sometimes, it carries this so far that it becomes comical: it says, "Why should I speak of oxen? the very shape of their backs makes it clear that they were not destined to carry burdens, whereas their necks were born for the yoke and their broad powerful shoulders for drawing the plough."[34] This is reminiscent of Pangloss' claim in Voltaire's *Candide* that Providence designed our nose to let us use eyeglasses. We design the yoke and plow to fit the oxen, just as we design eyeglasses to fit our noses.

The arguments in this work are clearly on a lower level than the arguments in the other works in this discourse, which is why we attribute it to a polemicist rather than to a philosopher. Yet the work does show a thorough knowledge of biology, and it is interesting as a review of the biological thought of the time.

Providence Cares for Plants and Animals

xlvii "To come now from things celestial to things terrestrial, which is there among these latter which does not clearly display the rational design of an intelligent being? In the first place, with the vegetation that springs from the earth, the stocks both give stability to the parts which they sustain and draw from the ground the sap to nourish the parts upheld by the roots; and the trunks are covered with bark or rind, the better to protect them against cold and heat. Again the vines cling to their props with their tendrils as with hands, and thus raise themselves erect like animals. Nay more, it is said that if planted near cabbages they shun them like pestle and noxious things, and will not touch them at any point.

33 *De Natura Deorum* II: lx.
34 *De Natura Deorum* II: lxiii.

"Again what a variety there is of animals, and what capacity they possess of persisting true to their various kinds! Some of them are protected by hides, others are clothed with fleeces, others bristle with spines; some we see covered with feathers, some with scales, some armed with horns, some equipped with wings to escape their foes. Nature, however, has provided with bounteous plenty for each species of animal that food which is suited to it. I might show in detail what provision has been made in the forms of the animals for appropriating and assimilating this food, how skilful and exact is the disposition of the various parts, how marvelous the structure of the limbs. For all the organs, at least those contained within the body, are so formed and so placed that none of them is superfluous or not necessary for the preservation of life. But nature has also bestowed upon the beasts both sensation and desire, the one to arouse in them the impulse to appropriate their natural foods, the other to enable them to distinguish things harmful from things wholesome.

"Again, some animals approach their food by walking, some by crawling, some by flying, some by swimming; and some seize their nutriment with their gaping mouth and with the teeth themselves, others snatch it in the grasp of their claws, others with their curved beaks, some suck, others graze, some swallow it whole, others chew it. Also some are of such lately stature that they easily reach their food upon the ground with their jaws; whereas the taller species, such as geese, swans, cranes and camels, are aided by the length of their necks; the elephant is even provided with a hand, because his body is so large that it was difficult for him to reach his food.

xlviii "Those beasts on the other hand whose mode of sustenance was to feed on animals of another species received from nature the gift either of strength or swiftness. Upon certain creatures there was bestowed even a sort of craft or cunning: for instance, one species of the spider tribe weaves a kind of net, in order to dispatch anything that is caught in it; another in order to . . . steadily corps watch, and, snatching anything that falls into it, devours it. The mussel, or *pina* as it is called in Greek, is a large bivalve which enters into a sort of Penelope with the tiny shrimp to procure food, and so, when little fishes swim into the gaping shell, the shrimp draws the attention of the mussel and the mussel shuts up its shells with a snap; thus two very dissimilar creatures obtain their food in common. In this case we are curious to know whether their association is due to a sort of mutual compact, or whether it was brought about by nature herself and goes back to the moment of their birth.

"Our wonder is also considerably excited by those aquatic animals which are born on land—crocodiles, for instance, and water-tortoises and certain snakes, which are born on dry land but as soon as they can first crawl make for the water. Again we often place ducks' eggs beneath hens, and the chicks that spring from the eggs are at first fed and mothered by the hens that hatched and reared them, but later on they leave their foster-mothers, and run away when they put up them, as soon as they have had the opportunity of seeing the water, their natural home. So powerful an instinct of self-preservation has nature implanted in living creatures.

xlix "I have even read in a book that there is a bird called the spoonbill, which procures its food by flying after those birds which dive in the sea, and upon their coming to the surface with a fish that they have caught, pressing their heads down with its beak until they drop their prey, which it pounces on for itself. It is also recorded of this bird that it is in the habit of gorging itself with shell-fish, which it digests by means of the heat of its stomach and then brings up again, and so picks out from them the parts that are good to eat. Sea-frogs again are said to be in the habit of covering themselves with sand and creeping along at the water's edge, and then when fishes approach them thinking they are something to eat, these are killed and devoured by the frogs. The kite and the crow live in a state of natural war as it were with one another, and therefore each destroys the other's eggs wherever it finds them.

"Another fact (observed by Aristotle, from whom most of these cases are cited) cannot but awaken our surprise, namely that cranes when crossing the seas on the way to warmer climates fly in a triangular formation. With the apex of the triangle they force aside the air in front of them, and then gradually on either side by means of their wings acting as oars the birds' onward flight is sustained, with the base of the triangle formed by the cranes gets the assistance of the wind when it is so to speak astern. The birds rest their necks and heads on the backs of those flying in front of them; and the leader, being himself unable to do this as he has no one to lean on, flies to the rear that he himself also may have a rest, while one of those already rested takes his place, and so they keep turns throughout the journey. I could adduce a number of similar instances, but you see the general idea. Another even better known classes of story illustrates the precautions taken by animals for their security, the watch they keep while feeding, their skill in hiding in their lairs.

1 "Other remarkable facts are that dogs cure themselves by vomiting and ibises in Egypt by purging — modes of treatment only recently, that is, a few generations ago, discovered by the talent of the medical profession. It has been reported that panthers, which in foreign countries are caught by means of poisoned meat, have a remedy which they employ to save themselves from dying; and that wild goats in Crete, when pierced with poisoned arrows, seek a herb called dittany, and on their swallowing this the arrows, it is said, drop out of their busy. Does, shortly before giving birth to their young, thoroughly purge themselves with a herb called hartwort. Again we observe how various species defend themselves against violence and danger with their own weapons, bulls with their horns, boars with their tusks, lions with their bite; some species protect themselves by flight, some by hiding, the cuttle-fish by emitting an inky fluid, the sting-ray by causing cramp, and also a number of creatures drive away their pursuers by their insufferably disgusting odor.

li "In order to secure the everlasting duration of the world-order, divine providence has made most careful provision to ensure the perpetuation of the families of animals and of trees and all the vegetable species. The latter all contain within them seed possessing the proprietor of multiplying the species; this seed is enclosed in the innermost part of the fruits that grow from each plant; and the same seeds supply mankind with an abundance of food, besides replenishing the earth with a fresh stock of plants of the same kind.

"Why should I speak of the amount of rational design displayed in animals to secure the perpetual preservation of their kind? To begin with some are male and some female, a device of nature to perpetuate the species. Then parts of their busy are most skillfully contrived to serve the purposes of procreation and of conception, and both male and female possess marvelous desires for copulation. And when the seed has settled in its place, it draws almost all the nutriment to itself and hedged within it fashions a living creature; when this has been dropped from the womb and has emerged, in the mammalian species almost all the nourishment received by the mother turns to milk, and the young just born, untaught and by nature's guidance, seek for the teats and satisfy their cravings with their bounty. And to show to us that none of these things merely happens by chance and that all are the work of nature's providence and skill, species that produce large litters of offspring, such as swine and dogs, have bestowed upon them a large number of teats, while those animals which bear only a few young have only a few teats. Why should I describe the affection shown by animals in rearing and protecting the offspring to which they have given birth, up to the point when they are able to defend themselves? although fishes, it is said, abandon their eggs when they have laid them, since these easily float and hatch out in the water.

lii "Turtles and crocodiles are said to lay their eggs on land and bury them and then go away, leaving their young to hatch and rear themselves. Hens and other birds find a quiet place in which to lay, and build themselves nests to sit on, covering these with the softest possible bedding in order to preserve the eggs most easily; and when they have hatched out their chicks they protect them by cherishing them with their wings so that they may not be injured by cold, and by shading them against the heat of the sun. When the young birds are able to use their sprouting wings, their mothers escort them in their flights, but are released from any further tendance upon them.

"Moreover the skill and industry of man also contribute to the preservation and security of certain animals and plants. For there are many species of both which could not survive without man's care.

"Also a plentiful variety of conveniences is found in different regions for the productive cultivation of the soil by man. Egypt is watered by the Nile, which corps the land completely flooded all the summer and afterwards retires leaving the soil soft and covered with mud, in readiness for sowing. Mesopotamia is fertilized by the Euphrates, which as it were imports into it new fields every year. The Indus, the largest river in the world, not only manures and softens the soil but actually sows it with seed, for it is said to bring down with it a great quantity of seeds resembling corn. And I could produce a number of other remarkable examples in a variety of places, and instance a variety of lands each prolific in a different kind of produce.

liii "But how great is the benevolence of nature, in giving birth to such an abundance and variety of delicious articles of food, and that not at one season only of the year, so that we have continually the delights of both novelty and plenty! How seasonable moreover and how some not for the human race alone but also for the animal and the various vegetable species is her gift of the Etesian winds![35] their breath moderates the excessive heat of summer, entirely also guide our ships across the sea upon a swift and steady course. Many instances must be passed over. For it is impossible to recount the conveniences afforded by rivers, the ebb and flow of the tides of the sea, the mountains

35 The relatively cool, dry summer winds that blow over the eastern Mediterranean from the north.

clothed with forests, the salt-beds lying far inland from the sea-coast, the copious stores of health-giving medicines that the earth contains, and all the countless arts necessary for livelihood and for life. Again the alternation of day and night contributes to the preservation of living creatures by affording one time for activity and another for repose. Thus every line of reasoning goes to prove that all things in this world of ours are marvelously governed by divine intelligence and wisdom for the safety and preservation of all.

Providence Cares for Man

"Here somebody will ask, for whose sake was all this vast system contrived? For the sake of the trees and plants, for these, though without sensation, have their sustenance from nature? But this at any rate is absurd. Then for the sake of the animals? It is no more likely that the gods took all this trouble for the sake of dumb, irrational creatures. For whose sake then shall one pronounce the world to have been created? Doubtless for the sake of those living beings which have the use of reason; these are the gods and mankind, who assuredly surpass all other things in excellence, since the most excellent of all things is reason. Thus we are led to believe that the world and all the things that it contains were made for the sake of gods and men.

liv "And that man has been cared for by divine providence will be more readily understood if we survey the whole structure of man and all the conformation and perfection of human nature.

There are three things requisite for the maintenance of animal life, food, drink and breath; and for the reception of all of these the mouth is most consummately adapted, receiving as it does an abundant supply of breath through the nostrils which communicate with it. The structure of the teeth within the mouth serves to chew the food, and it is divided up and softened by them. The front teeth are sharp, and bite our viands into pieces; the back teeth, called molars, masticate them, the process of mastication apparently being assisted also by the tongue. Next to the tongue comes the gullet, which is attached to its roots, and into which in the first place pass that substances that have been received in the mouth. The gullet is adjacent to the tonsils on either side of it, and reaches as far as the back or innermost part of the palate. The action and movements of the tongue drive and thrust the food down into the gullet, which receives it and drives it further down, the parts of the gullet below the food that is being swallowed dilating and the parts above it contracting. The windpipe, or trachea as it is termed by physicians, has an orifice attached to the roots of the tongue a little above the point where the tongue is joined to the gullet; it reaches to the lungs, and receives the air inhaled by breathing, and also exhales it and passes it out from the lungs; it is covered by a sort of lid, provided for the purpose of preventing a morsel of food from accidentally falling into it and impeding the breath.

Below the gullet lies the stomach, which is constructed as the receptacle of food and drink, whereas breath is inhaled by the lungs and heart. The stomach performs a number of remarkable operations; its structure consists principally of muscular fibers, and it is manifold and twisted; it compresses and contains the dry or moist nutriment that it receives, enabling it to be assimilated and digested; at one moment is constricted and at another relaxed, thus pressing and mixing together all that is passed into it, so that by means of the abundant heat which it possesses, and by its crushing the food, and also by the op of the breath, everything is digested and worked up so as to be easily distributed throughout the rest of the body.

lv "The lungs on the contrary are soft and of a loose and spongy consistency, well adapted to absorb the breath; which they inhale and exhale by alternately contracting and expanding, to provide frequent draughts of that aerial nutriment which is the chief support of animal life. The alimentary juice secreted from the rest of the food by the stomach flows from the bowels to the liver through certain ducts or channels reaching to the liver, to which they are attached, and connecting up what are called the doorways of the liver with the middle intestine. From the liver different channels pass in different directions, and through these falls the food passed down from the liver. From this food is secreted bile, and the liquids excreted by the kidneys; the residue turns into blood be flows to the aforesaid doorways of the liver, to which all its channels lead.

Flowing through these doorways the food at this very point pours into the so-called vena cava or hollow vein, and through this, being now completely worked up and digested, flows to the heart, and from the heart is distributed all over the body through a rather large number of veins that reach to every part of the frame. It would not be difficult to indicate the way in which the residue of the food is excreted by the alternate constriction and relaxation of the bowels; however this topic must be passed over lest my discourse should be somewhat offensive.

"Rather let me unfold the following instance of the incredible skillfulness of nature's handiwork. The air drawn into the lungs by breathing is warmed in the first instance by the breath itself and then by contact with the lungs; part of it is returned by the act of respiration, and part is received by a certain part of the heart called the cardiac ventricle, adjacent to which is a second similar vessel into which the blood flows from the liver three the vena cava mentioned above; and in this manner from these organs both the blood is diffused through the veins and the breath through the arteries all over the body. Both of these sets of vessels are very numerous and are closely interwoven with the tissues of the entire body; they testify to an extraordinary degree of skilful and divine craftsmanship.

"Why need I speak about the bones, which are the framework of the body? their marvelous cartilages are nicely adapted to secure stability, and fitted to end off the joints and to allow of movement and bodily activity of every sort. Add thereto the nerves or sinews which hold the joints together and whose ramifications pervade the entire body;

like the veins and arteries these lead from the heart as their starting-point and pass to all parts of the body.

lvi "Many further illustrations could be given of this wise and careful providence of nature, to illustrate the lavishness and splendor of the gifts bestowed by the gods on men. First, she has raised them from the ground to stand tall and upright, so that they might be able to behold the sky and so gain a knowledge of the gods. For men are sprung from the earth not as its inhabitants and denizens, but to be as it were the spectators of things supernal and heavenly, in the contemplation whereof no other species of animal participates.

"Next, the senses, posted in the citadel of the head as the reporters and messengers of the outer world, both in structure and position are marvelously adapted to their necessary services. The eyes as the watchmen have the highest station, to give them the widest outlook for the performance of their function. The ears also, having the duty of perceiving sound, the nature of which is to rise, are rightly placed in the upper part of the body. The nostrils likewise are rightly placed high inasmuch as all smells travel upwards, but also, because they have much to do with discriminating food and drink, they have with good reason been brought into the neighborhood of the mouth. Taste, which has the function of distinguishing the flavors of our various viands, is situated in that part of the face where nature has made an aperture for the passage of food and drink. The sense of touch is evenly diffused over all the body, to enable us to perceive all sorts of contacts and even the minutest impacts of both cold and heat. And just as architects relegate the drains of houses to the rear, away from the eyes and nose of the masters, since otherwise they would inevitably be somewhat offensive, so nature has banished the corresponding organs of the body far away from the neighborhood of the senses.

lvii "Again what artificer but nature, who is unsurpassed in her cunning, could have attained such skillfulness in the construction of the senses? First, she has clothed and walled the eyes with membranes of the finest texture, which she has made on the one hand transparent so that we may be able to see through them, and on the other hand firm of substance, to serve as the outer cover of the eye. The eyes she has made mobile and smoothly turning, so as both to avoid any threatened injury and to direct their gaze easily in any direction they desire. The actually organ of vision, called the pupil or 'little doll,'[36] is so small as easily to avoid objects that might injure it; and the lids, which are the covers of the eyes, are very soft to the touch so as not to hurt the pupil, and very neatly constructed as to be able both to shut the eyes in order that nothing may impinge upon them and to open them; and nature has provided that this process can be repeated again and again with extreme rapidity. The eyelids are furnished with a palisade of hairs, whereby to ward off any impinging object while the eyes are open, and so that while they are closed in sleep, when we do not need the eyes for seeing, they may be as it were tucked up for repose. Moreover the eyes are in advantageously retired position, and shielded on all sides by surrounding prominences; for first the parts above them are covered by the eyebrows which prevent sweat from flowing down from the scalp and forehead; then the cheeks, which are placed beneath them and which slightly project, protect them from below; and the nose is so placed as to seem to be a wall separating the eyes from one another.

"The organ of hearing on the other hand is always open, since we require this sense even when asleep, and when it receives a sound, we are aroused even from sleep. The auditory passage is winding, to prevent anything from being able to enter, as it might if the passage were clear and straight; it has further been provided that even the tiniest insect that may attempt to intrude may be caught in the sticky was of the ears. On the outside project the organs which we call ears, which are constructed both to cover and protect the sense-organ and to prevent the sounds that reach

36 Pūpilla, the Latin word for the pupil of the eye, literally means "little doll."

them from sliding past and being lost before they strike the sense. The apertures of the ears are hard and gristly, and much convoluted, because things with these qualities reflect and amplify sound; this is why tortoise-shell or horn gives resonance to a lyre, and always why winding passages and enclosures have an echo which is louder than the original sound. "Similarly the nostrils, which to serve the purposes required of them have to be always open, have narrower apertures, to prevent the entrance of anything that may harm them; and they are always moist, which is useful to guard them against dust and many other things. The sense of taste is admirably shielded, being enclosed in the mouth in a manner well suited for the performance of its function and for its protection against harm.

lviii "And all the senses of man far excel those of the lower animals. In the first place our eyes have a finer perception of many things in the arts which appeal to the sense of sight, painting, modeling and sculpture, and also in bodily movements and gestures; since the eyes judge beauty and arrangement and so to speak propriety of color and shape; and also other more important matters, for they also recognize virtues and vices, the angry and the friendly, the joyful and the sad, the brave man and the coward, the bold and the craven. The ears are likewise marvelously skilful organs of discrimination; they judge differences of tone, of pitch and of key in the music of the voice and of wind and stringed instruments, and many different qualities of voice, sonorous and dull, smooth and rough, bass and treble, flexible and hard, distinctions discriminated by the human ear alone. Likewise the nostrils, the taste and in some measure the touch have highly sensitive faculties of discrimination. And the arts invented to appeal to and indulge these senses are even more numerous than I could wish. The developments of perfumery and of the meretricious adornment of the person are obvious examples.

lix "Coming now to the actual mind and intellect of man, his reason, wisdom and foresight, one who cannot see that these owe their perfection to divine providence must in my view himself be devoid of these very faculties. While discussing this topic I could wish, Cotta, that I had the gift of your eloquence. How could not you describe first our powers of understanding, and then our faculty of conjoining premises and consequences in a single act of apprehension, the faculty I mean that enables us to judge what conclusion follows from any given propositions and to put the inference in syllogistic form, and also to delimit particular terms in a succinct definition; whence we arrive at an understanding of the potency and the nature of knowledge, which is the most excellent part even of the divine nature.

"Again, how remarkable are the faculties which you Academics invalidate and abolish, our sensory and intellectual perception and comprehension of external objects; it is by collating and comparing our precepts that we also create the arts that serve either practical necessities or the purpose of amusement.

"Then take the gift of speech, the queen of arts as you are fond of calling it—what a glorious, what a divine faculty it is! In the first place it enables us both to learn things we do not know and to teach things we do know to others; secondly it is our instrument for exhortation and persuasion, for consoling the afflicted and assuaging the fears of the terrified, for curbing passion and quenching appetite and anger; it is this that has united us in the bonds of justice, law and civil order, this that has sped us from savagery and barbarism. Now careful consideration will show that the mechanism of speech displays a skill on nature's part that surpasses belief. In the first place there is an artery passing from the lungs to the back of the mouth, which is the channel by which the voice, originating from the mind, is caught and uttered. Next, the tongue is placed in the mouth and confined by the teeth; it modulates and defines the inarticulate flow of the voice and renders its sounds district and clear by striking the teeth and other parts of the mouth. Accordingly my school is fond of comparing the tongue to the quill of a lyre, the teeth to the strings, and the nostrils to the horns which echo the notes of the strings when the instrument is played.

lx "Then what clever servants for a great variety of arts are the hands which nature has bestowed on man! The flexibility of the joints enables the fingers to close and open with equal ease, and to perform every motion without difficulty. Thus by the manipulation of the fingers the hand is enabled to paint, to model, to carve, and to draw forth the notes of the lyre and of the flute. And beside these arts of recreation there are those of utility, I mean agriculture and building, the weaving and stitching of garments, and the various modes of working bronze and iron; hence we realize that it was by applying the hand of the artificer to the discoveries of thought and observations of the senses that all our conveniences were attained, and we were enabled to have shelter, clothing and protection, and possessed cities, fortifications, houses and temples. Moreover men's industry, that is to say the work of their hands, procures us also our food in variety and abundance. It is the hand that gathers the divers products of the fields, whether to be consumed immediately or to be stored in repositories for the days to come; and our diet also includes flesh, fish and fowl, obtained partly by the chase and partly by breeding.

"We also tame the four-footed animals to carry us on their backs, their swiftness and strength bestowing strength and swiftness upon ourselves. We cause certain beasts to bear our burdens or to carry a yoke, we divert to our service the marvelously acute senses of elephants and the keen scent of hounds; we collect from the caves of the earth the iron which we need for tilling the land, we discover the deeply hidden veins of copper, silver and gold which serve us both for use and for adornment; we cut up a multitude of trees both wild and cultivated for timber which we employ partly by setting fire to it to warm our busy and cook our food, partly for building so as to shelter ourselves with houses and banish heat and cold. Timber moreover is of great value for constructing ships, whose voyages supply an abundance of sustenance of all sorts from all parts of the earth; and we alone have the power of controlling the most violent of nature's offspring, the sea and the winds, thanks to the science of navigation, and we use and enjoy many products of the sea. Likewise the entire command of the commodities produced on land is vested in mankind. We enjoy the fruits of the plains and of the mountains, the rivers and the lakes are ours, we sow corn, we plant trees, we fertilize the soil by irrigation, we confine the rivers and straighten or divert their courses. In fine, by means of our hands we essay to create as it were a second world within the world of nature.

lxi "Then moreover hasn't man's reason penetrated even to the sky? We alone of living creatures know the risings and settings and the courses of the stars, the human race has set limits to the day, the month and the year, and has learnt the eclipses of the sun and moon and foretold for all future time their occurrence, their extent and their dates. And contemplating the heavenly bodies the mind arrives at a knowledge of the gods, from which arises piety, with its comrades justice and the rest of the virtues, the sources of a life of happiness that vies with and resembles the divine existence and leaves us inferior to the celestial beings in nothing else save immortality, which is immaterial for happiness.

I think that my exposition of these matters has been sufficient to prove how widely man's nature surpasses all other living creatures; and this should make it clear that neither such a conformation and arrangement of the members nor such power of mind and intellect can possibly have been created by chance.

Nature Created for the Sake of Man

"It remains for me to show, in coming finally to a conclusion, that all the things in this world which men employ have been created and provided for the sake of men.

lxii "In the first place the world itself was created for the sake of gods and men, and the things that it contains were provided and contrived for the enjoyment of men. For the world is as it were the common dwelling-place of gods and men, or the city that belongs to both; for they alone have the use of reason and live by justice and by law. As therefore Athens and Sparta must be deemed to have been founded for the sake of the Athenians and the Spartans, and all the things contained in those cities are rightly said to belong to those peoples, so whatever things are contained in all the world must be deemed to belong to the gods and to men.

"Again the revolutions of the sun and moon no other heavenly bodies, although also contributing to the maintenance of the structure of the world, nevertheless also afford a spectacle for man to behold; for there is no sight of which it is more impossible to grow weary, none more beautiful nor displaying a more surpassing wisdom and skill; for by measuring the courses of the stars we know when the seasons will come round, and when their variations and changes will occur; and if these things are known to men alone, they must be judged to have been created for the sake of men.

"Then the earth, teeming with grain and vegetables of various kinds, which she pours forth in lavish abundance — does she appear to give birth to this produce for the sake of the wild beasts or for the sake of men? What shall I say of the vines and olives, whose bounteous and delightful fruits do not concern the lower animals at all? In fact the beasts of the field are entirely ignorant of the arts of sowing and cultivating, and of reaping and gathering the fruits of the earth in due season and storing them in garners; all these products are both enjoyed and tended by men.

lxiii "Just as therefore we are bound to say that lyres and flutes were made for the sake of those who can use them, so it must be agreed that the things of which I have spoken have been provided for those only who make use of them, and even if some portion of them is filched or plundered by some of the lower animals, we shall not admit that they were created for the sake of these animals also. Men do not store up corn for the sake of mice and ants but for their wives and

children and households; so the animals share these fruits of
the earth only by stealth as I have said, whereas the masters
enjoy them openly and freely.

It must therefore be admitted that all this abundance
was provided for the sake of men, unless perchance the
bounteous plenty and variety of our orchard fruit and the
delightfulness not only of its flavor but also of its scent and
appearance lead us to doubt whether nature intended this
gift for man alone! So far is it from being true that the furs
of the earth were provided for the sake of animals as well
as men, that the animals themselves, as we may see, were
created for the benefit of men. What other use have sheep
save that their fleeces are dressed and woven into clothing
for men? and in fact they could not have been reared nor
sustained nor have produced anything of value without
man's care and tendance. Then think of the dog, with its
trusty watchfulness, its fawning affection for its master
and hatred of strangers, its incredible keenness of scent in
following a trail and its eagerness in hunting—what do
these qualities imply except that they were created to serve
the conveniences of men? Why should I speak of oxen?
the very shape of their backs makes it clear that they were
not destined to carry burdens, whereas their necks were
born for the yoke and their broad powerful shoulders for
drawing the plough. And as it was by their means that the
earth was brought under tillage by breaking up its clods, no
violence was ever used towards them.... So valuable was
deemed the service that man received from oxen that to eat
their flesh was held a crime.

lxiv "It would be a long story to tell of the services
rendered by mules and asses, which were undoubtedly
created for the use of men. As for the pig, it can only furnish
food; indeed Chrysippus actually says that its soul was
given it to serve as salt and keep it from putrefaction; and
because this animal was fitted for the food of man, nature
made it the most prolific of all her offspring. Why should I
speak of the teeming swarms of delicious fish? or of birds,
which afford us so much pleasure that our Stoic Providence

appears to have been at times a disciple of Epicurus? and they could not even be caught save by man's intelligence and cunning;—although some birds, birds of flight and birds of utterance as our augurs call them, we believe to have been created for the purpose of giving omens. The great beasts of the forest again we take by hunting, both for food and in order to exercise ourselves in the mimic warfare of the chase, and also, as in the case of elephants, to train and discipline them for our employment, and to procure from their busy a variety of medicines for diseases and wounds, as also we do from certain roots and herbs whose values we have learnt by long-continued use and trial.

"Let the mind's eye survey the whole earth and all the seas, and you will behold now fruitful plains of measureless extent and mountains thickly clad with forests and pastures filled with flocks, now vessels sailing with marvelous swiftness across the sea. Nor only on the surface of the earth, but also in its darkest recesses there lurks an abundance of commodities which were created for men's use and which men alone discover.

5: On Divination
by an unknown Stoic author
from *De Natura Deorum* II: lxv-lxvi

Introduction

The brief and perfunctory argument for divination in this section is problematic. In the introduction to the discourse that contains these five works, Balbus says:

> To take a general view, the topic of the immortal gods which you raise is divided by our school into four parts: first they prove that the gods exist; next they explain their nature; then they show that the world is governed by them; and lastly that they care for the fortunes of mankind.[37]

After finishing with these four subjects, Cicero tacks on a fifth subject, divination, in this final section. The section is unified but seems improvised. At any rate, it serves as a good transition to the works about divination that follow, taken from Cicero's *De Divinatione*.

Divination

lxv "The next subject is one which each of you perhaps will seize upon for censure, Cotta because Carneades [the Academic Skeptic] used to enjoy tilting at the Stoics, Velleius because nothing provokes the ridicule of Epicurus so much as the art of prophecy; but in my view it affords the very strongest proof that man's welfare is studied by divine providence. I refer of course to Divination, which we see practiced in many regions and upon various matters and occasions both private and more especially public.

37 *De Natura Deorum* II: i.

Many observations are made by those who inspect the victims at sacrifices, many events are foreseen by augurs or revealed in oracles and prophecies, dreams and portents, a knowledge of which has often led to the acquisition of many things gratifying men's wishes and requirements, and also to the avoidance of many dangers. This power or art or instinct therefore has clearly been bestowed by the immortal gods on man, and on no other creature, for the ascertainment of future events.

"And if perchance these arguments separately fail to convince you, nevertheless in combination their collective weight will be bound to do so.

"Nor is the care and providence of the immortal gods bestowed only upon the human race in its entirety, but it is also wont to be extended to individuals. We may narrow down the entirety of the human race and bring it gradually down to smaller and smaller groups, and finally to single individuals.

lxvi "For if we believe, for the reasons that we have spoken of before, that the gods care for all human beings everywhere in every coast and region of the lands remote from this continent in which we dwell, then they care also for the men who inhabit with us these lands between the sunrise and the sunset. But if they care for these who inhabit that sort of vast island which we call the round earth, they also care for those who occupy continue divisions of that island, Europe, Asia and Africa. Therefore they also cherish the divisions of those divisions, for instance Rome, Athens, Sparta and Rhodes; and they cherish the individual citizens of those cities regarded separately from the whole body collectively …. It was this reason which drove the poets, and especially Homer, to attach to their chief heroes, Ulysses, Diomede, Agamemnon or Achilles, certain gods as the companions of their perils and adventures; moreover the gods have often appeared to men in person, as in the cases which I have mentioned above, so testifying that they care both for communities and for individuals.

And the same is proved by the portents of future

occurrences that are vouchsafed to men sometimes when they are asleep and sometimes when they are awake. Moreover we receive a number of warnings by means of signs and of the entrails of victims, and by many other things that long-continued usage has noted in such a manner as to create the art of divination. Therefore no great man ever existed who did not enjoy some portion of divine inspiration.

"Nor yet is this argument to be deprived by pointing to cases where a man's cornfields or vineyards have been damaged by a storm, or an accident has robbed him of some commodity of value, and inferring that the victim of one of these misfortunes is the object of god's hatred or neglect. The gods attend to great matters; they neglect small ones. Now great men always prosper in all their affairs, assuming that the teachers of our school and Socrates, the prince of philosophy, have satisfactorily discoursed upon the bounteous abundance of wealth that virtue bestows."

Conclusion to
Five Works on Nature and God
by Cicero
from *De Natura Deorum* II: lxvii

Introduction

Balbus briefly concludes his discourse by asking Cotta to mend his skeptical ways.

Cicero's Conclusion

lxvii "These are more or less the things that occurred to me which I thought proper to be said upon the subject of the nature of the gods. And for your part, Cotta, would you but listen to me, you would plead the same cause, and reflect that you are a leading citizen and a pontiff, and you would take advantage of the liberty enjoyed by your school of arguing both pro and contra to choose to espouse my side, and preferably to devote to this purpose those powers of eloquence which your rhetorical exercises have bestowed upon you and which the Academy has fostered. For the habit of arguing in support of atheism, whether it be done from conviction or in pretence, is a wicked and impious practice."

Two Stoic Works on Divination
From *De Divinatione* I: i-lvii

Introduction

Cicero's *De Divinatione* (*On Divination*) is framed as a dialog between Cicero, who uses arguments of the skeptical academy to debunk divination, and his brother Quintus Cicero, who uses arguments of the Stoics to defend divination.

Stoics distinguished between two types of divination. Divination by art is based on interpreting events such as entrails and natural portents, which require special skills to understand. Divination by nature happens automatically and does not require skill; its two major forms are divination in a frenzy and divination during dreams.

This discourse of Quintus Cicero in *De Divinatione* is clearly based on two separate source works. The first work is a coherent presentation of the Stoic case for divination, with discussions of divination by art and divination by nature followed with a general philosophical explanation of divination. The second work repeats points that were made in the first, including the division of the subject into divination by art and nature and the philosophical explanation of divination, and it is more disorganized than the first work.

Both works seem to have a great deal of Cicero's own writing added, rather than just being transcription of sources. There are many historical examples and examples from literature: Quintus even includes a long excerpt from Cicero's own poem "On My Consulship," which describes many portents that occurred when Cicero was consul. We have removed many of these examples to make the work more readable, but we must keep some because they are necessary to the argument. It is more difficult here than in most dialogs to tell what is from source works and what is by Cicero himself.

Cicero's Framing of the Two Works

i There is an ancient belief, handed down to us even from mythical times and firmly established by the general agreement of the Roman people and of all nations, that divination of some kind exists among men; this the Greeks call *mantikê* — that is, the foresight and knowledge of future events. A really splendid and helpful thing it is — if only such a faculty exists — since by its means men may approach very near to the power of gods. And, just as we Romans have done many other things better than the Greeks, so have we excelled them in giving to this most extraordinary gift a name, which we have derived from *divi*, a word meaning "gods," whereas, according to Plato's interpretation, they have derived it from *furor*, a word meaning "frenzy."

ii Now I am aware of no people, however refined and learned or however savage and ignorant, which does not think that signs are given of future events, and that certain persons can recognize those signs and foretell events before they occur. …

    …

iii Now my opinion is that, in sanctioning such usages, the ancients were influenced more by actual results than convinced by reason. However certain very subtle arguments to prove the trustworthiness of divination have been gathered by philosophers. Of these — to mention the most ancient — Xenophanes of Colophon, while asserting the existence of gods, was the only one who repudiated divination in its entirety; but all the others, with the exception of Epicurus, who babbled about the nature of the gods, approved of divination, though not in the same degree. For example, Socrates and all of the Socratic School, and Zeno and his followers, continued in the faith of the ancient philosophers and in agreement with the Old Academy and with the Peripatetics. Their predecessor, Pythagoras, who even wished to be considered an augur himself, gave the weight of his great name to the same practice; and that eminent author, Democritus, in many passages, strongly affirmed his belief in a presentiment of things to come. Moreover, Dicaearchus, the Peripatetic, though he accepted divination by dreams and frenzy, cast away all other kinds; and my intimate friend, Cratippus, whom I consider the peer of the greatest of the Peripatetics, also gave credence to the same kinds of divination but rejected the rest.

The Stoics, on the other hand (for Zeno in his writings had, as it were, scattered certain seed which Cleanthes had fertilized somewhat), defended nearly every sort of divination. Then came Chrysippus, a man of the keenest intellect, who exhaustively discussed the whole theory of divination in two books, and, besides, wrote one book on oracles and another on dreams. And following him, his pupil, Diogenes of Babylon, published one book, Antipater two, and my friend, Posidonius, five. But Panaetius, the teacher of Posidonius, a pupil, too, of Antipater, and, even a pillar of the Stoic school, wandered off from the Stoics, and, though he dared not say that there was no efficacy in divination, yet he did say that he was in doubt. Then, since the Stoics — much against their will I grant you — permitted this famous Stoic to doubt on one point will they not grant to us Academicians the right to do the same on all other points, especially since that about which Panaetius is not clear is clearer than the light of day to the other members of the Stoic school? At any rate, this praiseworthy tendency of the Academy to doubt has been approved by the solemn judgment of a most eminent philosopher.

iv Accordingly, since I, too, am in doubt as to the proper judgment to be rendered in regard to divination because of the many pointed and exhaustive arguments urged by Carneades against the Stoic view, and since I am afraid of giving a too hasty assent to a proposition which may turn out either false or insufficiently established, I have determined carefully and persistently to compare argument with argument just as I did in my three books On the Nature of the Gods. For a hasty acceptance of an erroneous opinion is discreditable in any case, and especially so in an inquiry as to how much weight should be given to auspices, to sacred rites, and to religious observances; for we run the risk of committing a crime against the gods if we disregard them, or of becoming involved in old women's superstition if we approve them.

v This subject has been discussed by me frequently on other occasions, but with somewhat more than ordinary care when my brother Quintus and I were together recently at my Tusculan villa. For the sake of a stroll we had gone to the Lyceum, which is the name of my upper gymnasium, when Quintus remarked:

"I have just finished a careful reading of the third book of your treatise, *On the Nature of the Gods*, containing Cotta's discussion, which, though it has shaken my views of religion, has not overthrown them entirely."

"Very good," said I; "for Cotta's argument is intended rather to refute the arguments of the Stoics than to destroy man's faith in religion."

Quintus then replied: "Cotta says the very same thing, and says it repeatedly, in order, as I think, not to appear to violate the commonly accepted canons of belief; yet it seems to me that, in his zeal to confute the Stoics, he utterly demolishes the gods. However, I am really at no loss for a reply to his reasoning; for in the second book Lucilius [Balbus] has made an adequate defense of religion and his argument, as you yourself state at the end of the third book, seemed to you nearer to the truth than Cotta's. But there is a question which you passed over in those books because, no doubt, you thought it more expedient to inquire into it in a separate discussion: I refer to divination, which is the foreseeing and foretelling of events considered as happening by chance. Now let us see, if you will, what efficacy it has and what its nature is. My own opinion is that, if the kinds of divination which we have inherited from our forefathers and now practice are trustworthy, then there are gods and, conversely, if there are gods then there are men who have the power of divination."

vi "Why, my dear Quintus," said I, "you are defending the very citadel of the Stoics in asserting the interdependence of these two propositions: 'if there is divination there are gods,' and, 'if there are gods there is divination.' But neither is granted as readily as you think. For it is possible that nature gives signs of future events without the intervention of a god, and it may be that there are gods without their having conferred any power of divination upon men."

To this he replied, "I, at any rate, find sufficient proof to satisfy me of the existence of the gods and of their concern in human affairs in my conviction that there are some kinds of divination which are clear and manifest. With your permission I will set forth my views on this subject, provided you are at leisure and have nothing else which you think should be preferred to such a discussion."

"Really, my dear Quintus," said I, "I always have time for philosophy. Moreover, since there is nothing else at this time that I can do with pleasure, I am all the more eager to hear what you think about divination."

1. On Divination
by an unknown Stoic author
From *De Divinatione* I: vii-xxxii

Introduction

This is a unified work that begins by dividing the subject into divination by art and divination by nature, discusses each of these two types of divination, and concludes with a philosophical defense of divination by nature based on the ideas of Cratippus.

Most of the defense of divination is based on examples rather than on philosophical arguments. Only the conclusion from Cratippus is philosophical. Thus, we attribute it to a Stoic author rather than to a Stoic philosopher.

In *De Divinatione*, this work is difficult to read because of the huge number of examples, many of which Cicero presumably added in his usual way. Here, we have removed many examples, making the work more readable.

Note that this work uses an argument from Cratippus, who was a Peripatetic, as well as from Stoics. Peripatetics believed only in divination by nature, not divination by art. For more about Cratippus' beliefs, see *Philosophy of Academic Skepticism*, where there is a criticism of Cratippus' defense of divination.

Two Types of Divination

"There is, I assure you," said he, "nothing new or original in my views; for those which I adopt are not only very old, but they are endorsed by the consent of all peoples and nations. There are two kinds of divination: the first is dependent on art, the other on nature. Now—to mention those almost entirely dependent on art—what nation or what state disregards the prophecies of soothsayers, or of interpreters of prodigies and lightnings, or of augurs, or of astrologers, or of oracles, or—to mention the two kinds which are classed as natural means of divination—the forewarnings of dreams, or of frenzy? Of these methods of divining it behooves us, I think, to examine the results rather than the causes. For there is a certain natural power, which now, through long-continued observation of signs and now, through some divine excitement and inspiration, makes prophetic announcement of the future.

Divination by Art

vii "Therefore let Carneades cease to press the question, which Panaetius also used to urge, whether Jove had ordered the crow to croak on the left side and the raven on the right. Such signs as these have been observed for an unlimited time, and the results have been checked and recorded. Moreover, there is nothing which length of time cannot accomplish and attain when aided by memory to receive and records to preserve. We may wonder at the variety of herbs that have been observed by physicians, of roots that are good for the bites of wild beasts, for eye affections, and for wounds, and though reason has never explained their force and nature, yet through their usefulness you have won approval for the medical art and for their discoverer.

"But come, let us consider instances, which although outside the category of divination, yet resemble it very closely:

> The heaving sea oft warns of coming storms,
> When suddenly its depths begin to swell;

viii "Your book, *Prognostics*, is full of such warning signs, but who can fathom their causes? And yet I see that the Stoic Boëthus has attempted to do so and has succeeded to the extent of explaining the phenomena of sea and sky. 14 But who can give a satisfactory reason why the following things occur?

Blue-grey herons, in fleeing the raging abyss of
the ocean,
Utter their warnings, discordant and wild, from
tremulous gullets,
Shrilly proclaiming that storms are impending
and laden with terrors.
Often at dawn, when Aurora releases the frost in
the dew-drops,
Does the nightingale pour from its breast
predictions of evil;
Then does it threaten and hurl from its throat its
incessant complaining.
Often the dark-hued crow, while restlessly
roaming the seashore,
Plunges its crest in the flood, as its neck encounters
the billows.
ix Hardly ever do we see such signs deceive us and
yet we do not see why it is so.
Ye, too, distinguish the signs, ye dwellers in
waters delightful,
When, with a clamor, you utter your cries that are
empty of meaning,
Stirring the fountains and ponds with absurd and
ridiculous croaking.

Who could suppose that frogs had this foresight? And yet
they do have by nature some faculty of premonition, clear
enough of itself, but too dark for human comprehension.
...

Now 'tis a fact that the evergreen mastic, e'er
burdened with leafage,
Thrice is expanding and budding and thrice
producing its berries;
Triple its signs for the purpose of showing three
seasons for ploughing.

Nor do I ever inquire why this tree alone blooms three
times, or why it makes the appearance of its blossoms
accord with the proper time for ploughing. I am content
with my knowledge that it does, although I may not know

why. Therefore, as regards all kinds of divination I will give the same answer that I gave in the cases just mentioned.

ₓ "I see the purgative effect of the scammony root and I see an antidote for snake-bite in the aristolochia plant — which, by the way, derives its name from its discoverer who learned of it in a dream — I see their power and that is enough; why they have it I do not know. Thus as to the cause of those premonitory signs of winds and rains already mentioned I am not quite clear, but their force and effect I recognize, understand, and vouch for. Likewise as to the cleft or thread in the entrails: I accept their meaning; I do not know their cause. And life is full of individuals in just the same situation that I am in, for nearly everybody employs entrails in divining. Again: is it possible for us to doubt the prophetic value of lightning? Have we not many instances of its marvels? ...

[We omit a long passage quoting Cicero's poem "My Consulship," about portents that occurred when he was consul and of other prophesies.]

xiii ".... In view, therefore, of your acts, and in view too of your own verses which I have quoted and which were composed with the utmost care, could you be persuaded to controvert the position which I maintain in regard to divination?

"But what? You ask, Carneades, do you, why these things so happen, or by what rules they may be understood? I confess that I do not know, but that they do so fall out I assert that you yourself see. 'Mere accidents,' you say. Now, really, is that so? Can anything be an 'accident' which bears upon itself every mark of truth? Four dice are cast and a Venus throw³⁸ results — that is chance; but do you think it would be chance, too, if in one hundred casts you made one hundred Venus throws? It is possible for paints flung at random on a canvas to form the outlines of a face; but do you imagine that an accidental scattering of pigments could produce the beautiful portrait of Venus of Cos? Suppose that a hog should form the letter 'A' on the ground with its

38 The best throw in the Roman game of knucklebones.

snout; is that a reason for believing that it would write out Ennius' poem The Andromache?

"Carneades used to have a story that once in the Chian quarries when a stone was split open there appeared the head of the infant god Pan; I grant that the figure may have borne some resemblance to the god, but assuredly the resemblance was not such that you could ascribe the work to a Scopas. For it is undeniably true that no perfect imitation of a thing was ever made by chance.

xiv " 'But,' it is objected, 'sometimes predictions are made which do not come true.' And pray what art — and by art I mean the kind that is dependent on conjecture and deduction — what art, I say, does not have the same fault? Surely the practice of medicine is an art, yet how many mistakes it makes! And pilots — do they not make mistakes at times? ... Then, did the fact that so many illustrious captains and kings suffered shipwreck deprive navigation of its right to be called an art? And is military science of no effect because a general of the highest renown recently lost his army and took to flight?[39] Again, is statecraft devoid of method or skill because political mistakes were made many times ...? So it is with the responses of soothsayers, and, indeed, with every sort of divination whose deductions are merely probable; for divination of that kind depends on inference and beyond inference it cannot go. It sometimes misleads perhaps, but none the less in most cases it guides us to the truth. For this same conjectural divination is the product of boundless eternity and within that period it has grown into an art through the repeated observation and record of almost countless instances in which the same results have been preceded by the same signs.

...

xvi "In ancient times scarcely any matter out of the ordinary was undertaken, even in private life, without first consulting the auspices, clear proof of which is given even at the present time by our custom of having 'nuptial auspices,' though they have lost their former religious significance

39 Pompey, who was defeated by Caesar at Pharsalus in 48 BC.

and only preserve the name. For just as to-day on important occasions we make use of entrails in divining—though even they are employed to a less extent than formerly—so in the past resort was usually had to divination by means of birds. And thus it is that by failing to seek out the unpropitious signs we run into awful disasters. ....

....

Divination by Nature

xviii "I agree, therefore, with those who have said that there are two kinds of divination: one, which is allied with art; the other, which is devoid of art. Those diviners employ art, who, having learned the known by observation, seek the unknown by deduction. On the other hand those do without art who, unaided by reason or deduction or by signs which have been observed and recorded, forecast the future while under the influence of mental excitement, or of some free and unrestrained emotion. This condition often occurs to men while dreaming and sometimes to persons who prophesy while in a frenzy—like Bacis of Boeotia, Epimenides of Crete and the Sibyl of Erythraea. In this latter class must be placed oracles—not oracles given by means of 'equalized lots'—but those uttered under the impulse of divine inspiration; although divination by lot is not in itself to be despised, if it has the sanction of antiquity, as in the case of those lots which, according to tradition, sprang out of the earth; for in spite of everything, I am inclined to think that they may, under the power of God, be so drawn as to give an appropriate response. Men capable of correctly interpreting all these signs of the future seem to approach very near to the divine spirit of the gods whose wills they interpret, just as scholars do when they interpret the poets.

"What sort of cleverness is it, then, that would attempt by sophistry to overthrow facts that antiquity has established? I fail—you tell me—to discover their cause. That, perhaps, is one of Nature's hidden secrets. God has not willed me to know the cause, but only that I should use the means which he has given. Therefore, I will use them and I will not allow myself to be persuaded that the whole Etruscan nation has gone stark mad on the subject of entrails, or that these same people are in error about lightnings, or that they are false interpreters of portents; for many a time the rumblings and roarings and quakings of the earth have given to our republic and to other states certain forewarnings of subsequent disaster. ...

...

xix ".... Speaking now of natural divination, everybody knows the oracular responses which the Pythian Apollo gave to Croesus, to the Athenians, Spartans, Tegeans, Argives, and Corinthians. Chrysippus has collected a vast number of these responses, attested in every instance by abundant proof. But I pass them by as you know them well. I will urge only this much, however, in defense: the oracle at Delphi never would have been so much frequented, so famous, and so crowded with offerings from peoples and kings of every land, if all ages had not tested the truth of its prophecies. For a long time now that has not been the case. Therefore, as at present its glory has waned because it is no longer noted for the truth of its prophecies, so formerly it would not have enjoyed so exalted a reputation if it had not been trustworthy in the highest degree. Possibly, too, those subterraneous exhalations which used to kindle the soul of the Pythian priestess with divine inspiration have gradually vanished in the long lapse of time; just as within our own knowledge some rivers have dried up and disappeared, while others, by winding and twisting, have changed their course into other channels. But explain the decadence of the oracle as you wish, since it offers a wide field for discussion, provided you grant what cannot be denied without distorting the entire record of history, that the oracle at Delphi made true prophecies for many hundreds of years.

xx "But let us leave oracles and come to dreams. In his treatise on this subject Chrysippus, just as Antipater does, has assembled a mass of trivial dreams which he explains according to Antiphon's rules of interpretation. The work, I admit, displays the acumen of its author, but it would have been better if he had cited illustrations of a more serious type. Now, Philistus, who was a learned and painstaking man and a contemporary of the times of which he writes, gives us the following story of the mother of Dionysius, the tyrant of Syracuse: while she was with child and was carrying this same Dionysius in her womb, she dreamed that she had been delivered of an infant satyr. When she referred this dream to the interpreters of portents, who in Sicily were called 'Galeotae,' they replied, so Philistus relates, that she should bring forth a son who would be very eminent in Greece and would enjoy a long and prosperous career.

...

xxiii ".... Why need I bring forth from Dinon's Persian annals the dreams of that famous prince, Cyrus, and their interpretations by the magi? But take this instance: Once upon a time Cyrus dreamed that the sun was at his feet. Three times, so Dinon writes, he vainly tried to grasp it and each time it turned away, escaped him, and finally disappeared. He was told by the magi, who are classed as wise and learned men among the Persians, that his grasping for the sun three times portended that he would reign for thirty years. And thus it happened; for he lived to his seventieth year, having begun to reign at forty.

"It certainly must be true that even barbarians have some power of foreknowledge and of prophecy ....

xxv "We read in Plato that Socrates, while in prison, said in a conversation with his friend Crito: 'I am to die in three days; for in a dream I saw a woman of rare beauty, who called me by name and quoted this verse from Homer:

> Gladly on Phthia's shore the third day's dawn
> shall behold thee.'

And history informs us that his death occurred as he had foretold. That disciple of Socrates, Xenophon—and what a man he was!—records the dreams he had during his campaign with Cyrus the Younger, and their remarkable fulfillment. Shall we say that Xenophon is either a liar or a madman?

…

xxvii "And who, pray, can make light of the two following dreams which are so often recounted by Stoic writers? The first one is about Simonides, who once saw the dead body of some unknown man lying exposed and buried it. Later, when he had it in mind to go on board a ship he was warned in a vision by the person to whom he had given burial not to do so and that if he did he would perish in a shipwreck. Therefore he turned back and all the others who sailed were lost.

"The second dream is very well known and is to this effect: Two friends from Arcadia who were taking a journey together came to Megara, and one traveler put up at an inn and the second went to the home of a friend. After they had eaten supper and retired, the second traveler, in the dead of the night, dreamed that his companion was imploring him to come to his aid, as the innkeeper was planning to kill him. Greatly frightened at first by the dream he arose, and later, regaining his composure, decided that there was nothing to worry about and went back to bed. When he had gone to sleep the same person appeared to him and said: 'Since you would not help me when I was alive, I beg that you will not allow my dead body to remain unburied. I have been killed by the innkeeper, who has thrown my body into a cart and covered it with dung. I pray you to be at the city gate in the morning before the cart leaves the town,' Thoroughly convinced by the second dream he met the cart-driver at the gate in the morning, and, when he asked what he had in the cart, the driver fled in terror. The Arcadian then removed his friend's dead body from the cart, made complaint of the crime to the authorities, and the innkeeper was punished. What stronger proof of a divinely inspired dream than this can be given?

…

xxix " 'Ah,' it is objected, 'but many dreams are untrustworthy.' Rather, perhaps, their meaning is hidden from us. But grant that some are untrustworthy, why do we declaim against those that trustworthy? The fact is the latter would be much more frequent if we went to our rest in proper condition. But when we are burdened with food and drink our dreams are troubled and confused. Observe what Socrates says in Plato's *Republic*:

> "When a man goes to sleep, having the thinking and reasoning portion of his soul languid and inert, but having that other portion, which has in it a certain brutishness and wild savagery, immoderately gorged with drink and food, then does that latter portion leap up and hurl itself about in sleep without check. In such a case every vision presented to the mind is so devoid of thought and reason that the sleeper dreams that he is committing incest with his mother, or that he is having unlawful commerce indiscriminately with gods and men, and frequently too, with beasts; or even that he is killing someone and staining his hands with impious bloodshed; and that he is doing many vile and hideous things recklessly and without shame. But, on the other hand, when the man, whose habits of living and of eating are wholesome and temperate, surrenders himself to sleep, having the thinking and reasoning portion of his soul eager and erect, and satisfied by a feast of noble thoughts, and having that portion which feeds on carnal pleasures neither utterly exhausted by abstinence nor cloyed by over-indulgence—for, as a rule, the edge of thought is dulled whether nature is starved or overfed—and, when such a man, in addition, has that third portion of the soul, in which the fire of anger burns, quieted and subdued—thus having the two irrational portions under complete control—then will the thinking and reasoning portion of his soul shine forth and show itself keen and strong

for dreaming and then will his dreams be peaceful
and worthy of trust.

I have reproduced Plato's very words.

xxx "Then shall we listen to Epicurus rather than to Plato?
As for Carneades, in his ardor for controversy he asserts
this and now that. 'But,' you retort, 'Epicurus says what he
thinks.' But he thinks nothing that is ever well reasoned, or
worthy of a philosopher. Will you, then, put this man before
Plato or Socrates, who though they gave no reason, would
yet prevail over these petty philosophers by the mere weight
of their name? Now Plato's advice to us is to set out for the
land of dreams with bodies so prepared that no error or
confusion may assail the soul. For this reason, it is thought,
the Pythagoreans were forbidden to indulge in beans; for
that food produces great flatulence and induces a condition
at war with a soul in search for truth. When, therefore, the
soul has been withdrawn by sleep from contact with sensual
ties, then does it recall the past, comprehend the present,
and foresee the future. For though the sleeping body then
lies as if it were dead, yet the soul is alive and strong, and
will be much more so after death when it is wholly free
of the body. Hence its power to divine is much enhanced
by the approach of death. For example, those in the grasp
of a serious and fatal sickness realize the fact that death
impends; and so, visions of dead men generally appear to
them and then their desire for fame is strongest; while those
who have lived otherwise than as they should, feel, at such
a time, the keenest sorrow for their sins.

"Moreover, proof of the power of dying men to prophesy
is also given by Posidonius in his well-known account of a
certain Rhodian, who, when on his death-bed, named six
men of equal age and foretold which of them would die
first, which second, and so on. Now Posidonius holds the
view that there are three ways in which men dream as the
result of divine impulse: first, the soul is clairvoyant of itself
because of its kinship with the gods; second, the air is full
of immortal souls, already clearly stamped, as it were, with

the marks of truth; and third, the gods in person converse with men when they are asleep. And, as I said just now, it is when death is at hand that men most readily discern signs of the future. ...

xxxi "It is clear that, in our ordinary speech, we should not have made such frequent use of the word *praesagire*, meaning 'to sense in advance, or to presage,' if the power of presaging had been wholly non-existent. ... Now *sagire* means 'to have a keen perception.' Accordingly certain old women are called *sagae*, because they are assumed to know a great deal, and dogs are said to be 'sagacious.' And so one who has knowledge of a thing before it happens is said to 'presage,' that is, to perceive the future in advance.

"Therefore the human soul has an inherent power of presaging or of foreknowing infused into it from without, and made a part of it by the will of God. If that power is abnormally developed, it is called 'frenzy' or 'inspiration,' which occurs when the soul withdraws itself from the body and is violently stimulated by a divine impulse ....

...

Cratippus on Divination by Nature

xxxii ".... As briefly as I could, I have discussed divination by means of dreams and frenzy, which, as I said, are devoid of art. Both depend on the same reasoning, which is that habitually employed by our friend Cratippus: 'The human soul is in some degree derived and drawn from a source exterior to itself. Hence we understand that outside the human soul there is a divine soul from which the human soul is sprung. Moreover, that portion of the human soul which is endowed with sensation, motion, and carnal desire is inseparable from bodily influence; while that portion which thinks and reasons is most vigorous when it is most distant from the body. And so, after giving examples of true prophecies through frenzy and dreams, Cratippus usually concludes his argument in this way:

" 'Though without eyes it is impossible to perform the

act and function of sight, and though the eyes sometimes cannot perform their appointed function, yet when a person has even once so employed his eyes as to see things as they are, he has a realization of what correct vision is. Likewise, therefore, although without the power of divination it is impossible for the act and function of divining to exist, and though one with that power may sometimes be mistaken and may make erroneous prophecies, yet it is enough to establish the existence of divination that a single event has been so clearly foretold as to exclude the hypothesis of chance. But there are many such instances; therefore, the existence of divination must be conceded.'

2. On Divination
by Cicero and unknown Stoic authors
From *De Divinatione* I: xxxiii-lvii

Introduction

This continuation of Quintus' discourse is clearly from a second source work, because it repeats points already made, and because the earlier part of his discourse is complete in itself, having covered divination by art and nature, as it promised to do at the beginning.

Cicero begins this section of the discourse by starting all over again, even admitting that he has talked about this before:

> But those methods of divination which are dependent on conjecture, or on deductions from events previously observed and recorded, are, as I have said before, not natural, but artificial, and include the inspection of entrails, augury, and the interpretation of dreams. These are disapproved of by the Peripatetics and defended by the Stoics.

This second work also repeats arguments already made in the first. For instance, it says,

> For example, if I were to say that the magnet attracted iron and drew it to itself, and I could not tell you why, then I suppose you would utterly deny that the magnet had any such power.[40]

while the first work makes the same point by saying:

> "I see the purgative effect of the scammony root and I see an antidote for snake-bite in the aristolochia ...I see their power and that is enough;

why they have it I do not know. Thus as to the cause of those premonitory signs of winds and rains already mentioned I am not quite clear, but their force and effect I recognize, understand, and vouch for. Likewise as to the cleft or thread in the entrails: I accept their meaning; I do not know their cause.[41]

As the first work ends with a philosophical justification of divination by nature from Cratippus, this second work ends with a philosophical justification of divination by nature and by art from Posidonius.

This second work is much less coherent than the first. It does have a main sections about divination by art and divination by nature. But there are digressions and subsections about divination by nature within the main section about divination by art, and also subsections about divination by art within the main section about divination by nature. Thus, it seems likely that Cicero pieced it together from a number of different sources. The individual sources are too short to stand on their own, so we are treating this as a single work by Cicero and the unknown Stoic authors who wrote the source works that he has pieced together.

Divination by Art

xxxiii "But those methods of divination which are dependent on conjecture, or on deductions from events previously observed and recorded, are, as I have said before, not natural, but artificial, and include the inspection of entrails, augury, and the interpretation of dreams. These are disapproved of by the Peripatetics and defended by the Stoics. Some are based upon records and usage, as is evident from the Etruscan books on divination by means of inspection of entrails and by means of thunder and lightning, and as is also evident from the books of your augural college; while others are dependent on conjecture made suddenly and on the spur of the moment. An instance

41 *De Divinatione* I: viii.

of the latter kind is that of Calchas in Homer, prophesying the number of years of the Trojan War from the number of sparrows.

...

xxxvi "Trustworthy conjectures in divining are made by experts. For instance, when Midas, the famous king of Phrygia, was a child, ants filled his mouth with grains of wheat as he slept. It was predicted that he would be a very wealthy man; and so it turned out. Again, while Plato was an infant, asleep in his cradle, bees settled on his lips and this was interpreted to mean that he would have a rare sweetness of speech. Hence in his infancy his future eloquence was foreseen.

Digression on Other Sorts of Inspiration

[Note that, though it is in the main section about divination by art, this digression is mostly about divination by nature, beginning with the frenzy of the priestess of Delphi, a prime example of divination by nature.]

"Then what do we expect? Do we wait for the immortal gods to converse with us in the forum, on the street, and in our homes? While they do not, of course, present themselves in person, they do diffuse their power far and wide—sometimes enclosing it in caverns of the earth and sometimes imparting it to human beings. The Pythian priestess at Delphi was inspired by the power of the earth92 and the Sibyl by that of nature. ...

xxxvii "And poetic inspiration also proves that there is a divine power within the human soul. Democritus says that no one can be a great poet without being in a state of frenzy, and Plato says the same thing. Let Plato call it 'frenzy' if he will, provided he praises it as it was praised in his Phaedrus. And what about your own speeches in law suits. Can the delivery of you lawyers be impassioned, weighty, and fluent unless your soul is deeply stirred? Upon my word, many a time have I seen in you such passion of look and gesture that I thought some power was rendering you unconscious of what you did; and, if I may cite a less striking example, I have seen the same in your friend Aesopus.

"Frequently, too, apparitions present themselves and, though they have no real substance, they seem to have.

xxxviii "Aristotle thought that even the people who rave from the effects of sickness and are called 'hypochondriacs' have within their souls some power of foresight and of prophecy. But, for my part, I am inclined to think that such a power is not to be distributed either to a diseased stomach or to a disordered brain. On the contrary, it is the healthy soul and not the sickly body that has the power of divination.

The Stoics' Philosophical Argument for Divination by Art

"The Stoics, for example, establish the existence of divination by the following process of reasoning:

" 'If there are gods and they do not make clear to man in advance what the future will be, then they do not love man; or, they themselves do not know what the future will be; or, they think that it is of no advantage to man to know what it will be; or, they think it inconsistent with their dignity to give man forewarnings of the future; or, finally, they, though gods, cannot give intelligible signs of coming events. But it is not true that the gods do not love us, for they are the friends and benefactors of the human race; nor is it true that they do not know their own decrees and their own plans; nor is it true that it is of no advantage to us to know what is going to happen, since we should be more prudent if we knew; nor is it true that the gods think it inconsistent with their dignity to give forecasts, since there is no more excellent quality than kindness; nor is it true that they have not the power to know the future; therefore it is not true that there are gods and yet that they do not give us signs of the future; but there are gods, therefore they give us such signs; and if they give us such signs, it is not true that they give us no means to understand those signs — otherwise their signs would be useless; and if they give us the means, it is not true that there is no divination; therefore there is divination.'

Defense of Divination Continued

xxxix "Chrysippus, Diogenes, and Antipater employ the same reasoning. Then what ground is there to doubt the absolute truth of my position? For I have on my side reason, facts, peoples, and races, both Greek and barbarian, our own ancestors, the unvarying belief of all ages, the greatest philosophers, the poets, the wisest men, the builders of cities, and the founders of republics. Are we not satisfied with the unanimous judgment of men, and do we wait for beasts to give their testimony too? The truth is that no other argument of any sort is advanced to show the futility of the various kinds of divination which I have mentioned except the fact that it is difficult to give the cause or reason of every kind of divination.

"You ask why everything happens. You have a perfect right to ask, but that is not the point at issue now. The question is, Does it happen, or does it not? For example, if I were to say that the magnet attracted iron and drew it to itself, and I could not tell you why, then I suppose you would utterly deny that the magnet had any such power. At least that is the course you pursue in regard to the existence of the power of divination, although it is established by our reading and by the traditions of our forefathers. Why, even before the dawn of philosophy, which is a recent discovery, the average man had no doubt about divination, and, since its development, no philosopher of any sort of reputation has had any different view. I have already cited Pythagoras, Democritus, and Socrates and, of the ancients, I have excluded no one except Xenophanes. To them I have added the Old Academy, the Peripatetics, and the Stoics. The only dissenter is Epicurus. But why wonder at that? for is his opinion of divination any more discreditable than his view that there is no such thing as a disinterested virtue?

...

Digression on Divination by Art in Different Countries

xlii "Now, for my part, I believe that the character of the country determined the kind of divination which its inhabitants adopted. For example, the Egeans and Babylonians, who live on the level surface of open plains, with no hills to obstruct a view of the sky, have devoted their attention wholly to astrology. But the Etruscans, being in their nature of a very ardent religious temperament and accustomed to the frequent sacrifice of victims, have given their chief attention to the study of entrails. And as on account of the density of the atmosphere signs from heaven were common among them, and furthermore since that atmospheric condition caused many phenomena both of earth and sky and also certain prodigies that occur in the conception and birth of men and cattle — for these reasons the Etruscans have become very proficient in the interpretation of portents. Indeed, the inherent force of these means of divination, as you like to observe, is clearly shown by the very words so aptly chosen by our ancestors to describe them. Because they 'make manifest' (*ostendunt*), 'portend' (*portendunt*), 'intimate' (*monstrant*), 'predict' (*praedicunt*), they are called 'manifestations,' 'portents,' 'intimations,' and 'prodigies.' But the Arabians, Phrygians, and Cilicians, being chiefly engaged in the rearing of cattle, are constantly wandering over the plains and mountains in winter and summer and, on that account, have found it quite easy to study the songs and flight of birds. The same is true of the Pisidians and of our fellow-countrymen, the Umbrians. While the Carians, and especially the Telmessians, already mentioned, because they live in a country with a very rich and prolific soil, whose fertility produces many abnormal growths, have turned their attention to the study of prodigies.

xliii "But who fails to observe that auspices and all other kinds of divination flourish best in the best regulated states? And what king or people has there ever been who did not employ divination? I do not mean in time of peace only, but much more even in time of war, when the strife and struggle for safety is hardest. ...

...

Conclusion of Defense of Divination by Art

il "But let us bring the discussion back to the point from which it wandered. Assume that I can give no reason for any of the instances of divination which I have mentioned and that I can do no more than show that they did occur, is that not a sufficient answer to Epicurus and to Carneades? And what does it matter if, as between artificial and natural divination, the explanation of the former is easy and of the latter is somewhat hard? For the results of those artificial means of divination, by means of entrails, lightnings, portents, and astrology, have been the subject of observation for a long period of time. But in every field of inquiry great length of time employed in continued observation begets an extraordinary fund of knowledge, which may be acquired even without the intervention or inspiration of the gods, since repeated observation makes it clear what effect follows any given cause, and what sign precedes any given event.

Divination by Nature

"The second division of divination, as I said before, is the natural; and it, according to exact teaching of physics, must be ascribed to divine Nature, from which, as the wisest philosophers maintain, our souls have been drawn and poured forth. And since the universe is wholly filled with the Eternal Intelligence and the Divine Mind, it must be that human souls are influenced by their contact with divine souls. But when men are awake their souls, as a rule, are subject to the demands of everyday life and are withdrawn from divine association because they are hampered by the chains of the flesh.

"However, there is a certain class of men, though small in number, who withdraw themselves from carnal influences and are wholly possessed by an ardent concern for the contemplation of things divine.

Digression on Other Forms of Prediction

[Notice that, though it is in the main section about

divination by nature, this digression is about forms of divination by art.]

"Some of these men make predictions, not as the result of direct heavenly inspiration, but by the use of their own reason. For example, by means of natural law, they foretell certain events, such as a flood, or the future destruction of heaven and earth by fire. Others, who are engaged in public life, like Solon of Athens, as history describes him, discover the rise of tyranny long in advance. Such men we may call 'foresighted' — that is, 'able to foresee the future'; but we can no more apply the term 'divine' to them than we can apply it to Thales of Miletus, who, as the story goes, in order to confound his critics and thereby show that even a philosopher, if he sees fit, can make money, bought up the entire olive crop in the district of Miletus before it had begun to bloom. Perhaps he had observed, from some personal knowledge he had on the subject, that the crop would be abundant. And, by the way, he is said to have been the first man to predict the solar eclipse which took place in the reign of Astyages.

1 "There are many things foreseen by physicians, pilots, and also by farmers, but I do not call the predictions of any of them divination. I do not even call that a case of divination when Anaximander, the natural philosopher, warned the Spartans to leave the city and their homes and to sleep in the fields under arms, because an earthquake was at hand. Then the whole city fell down in ruins and the extremity of Mount Taygetus was torn away like the stern of a ship in a storm. Not even Pherecydes, the famous teacher of Pythagoras, will be considered a prophet because he predicted an earthquake from the appearance of some water drawn from an unfailing well.

Divination by Nature Continued

"In fact, the human soul never divines naturally, except when it is so unrestrained and free that it has absolutely no association with the body, as happens in the case of frenzy and of dreams. Hence both these kinds of divination have been sanctioned by Dicaearchus and also, as I said, by our friend Cratippus. Let us grant that these two methods (because they originate in nature) take the highest rank in divination; but we will not concede that they are the only kind. But if, on the other hand, Dicaearchus and Cratippus believe that there is nothing in observation, they hold a doctrine destructive of the foundation on which many things in everyday life depend. However, since these men make us some concession—and that not a small one—in granting us divination by frenzy and dreams, I see no cause for any great war with them, especially in view of the fact that there are some philosophers who do not accept any sort of divination whatever.

"Those then, whose souls, spurning their bodies, take wings and fly abroad—inflamed and aroused by a sort of passion—these men, I say, certainly see the things which they foretell in their prophecies. Such souls do not cling to the body and are kindled by many different influences. For example, some are aroused by certain vocal tones, as by Phrygian songs, many by groves and forests, and many others by rivers and seas. I believe, too, that there were certain subterranean vapors which had the effect of inspiring persons to utter oracles.

li "Such is the rationale of prophecy by means of frenzy, and that of dreams is not much unlike it. For the revelations made to seers when awake are made to us in sleep. While we sleep and the body lies as if dead, the soul is at its best, because it is then freed from the influence of the physical senses and from the worldly cares that weigh it down. And since the soul has lived from all eternity and has had converse with numberless other souls, it sees everything that exists in nature, provided that moderation and restraint have been used in eating and in drinking, so that the soul is in a condition to watch while the body sleeps. Such is the explanation of divination by dreams.

Digression on Antiphon's Theory of Dream Interpretation

"At this point it is pertinent to mention Antiphon's well-known theory of the interpretation of dreams. His view is that the interpreters of dreams depending upon technical skill and not upon inspiration. He has the same view as to the interpretation of oracles and of frenzied utterances; for they all have their interpreters, just as poets have their commentators. Now it is clear that divine nature would have done a vain thing if she had merely created iron, copper, silver, and gold and had not shown us how to reach the veins in which those metals lie; the gift of field crops and orchard fruits would have been useless to the human race without a knowledge of how to cultivate them and prepare them for food; and building material would be of no service without the carpenter's art to convert it into lumber. So it is with everything that the gods have given for the advantage of mankind, there has been joined some art whereby that advantage may be turned to account. The same is true of dreams, prophecies, and oracles: since many of them were obscure and doubtful, resort was had to the skill of professional interpreters.

Philosophical Justification of Divination by Art

[Though it is in the main section about divination by nature, this subsection is actually about divination by art, about understanding signs. It can be read as a continuation of the digression about Antiphon's theory.]

"Now there is a great problem as to how prophets and dreamers can see things, which, at the time, have no actual existence anywhere. But that question would be solved quite readily if we were to investigate certain other questions which demand consideration first. For the theory in regard to the nature of the gods, so clearly developed in the second book of your work on that subject, includes this whole question. If we maintain that theory we shall establish the very point which I am trying to make: namely, 'that there are gods; that they rule the universe by their foresight; and that they direct the affairs of men—not merely of men in the mass, but of each individual.' If we succeed in holding that position—and for my part I think it impregnable—then surely it must follow that the gods give to men signs of coming events.

lii "But it seems necessary to settle the principle on which these signs depend. For, according to the Stoic doctrine, the gods are not directly responsible for every fissure in the liver or for every song of a bird; since, manifestly, that would not be seemly or proper in a god and furthermore is impossible. But, in the beginning, the universe was so created that certain results would be preceded by certain signs, which are given sometimes by entrails and by birds, sometimes by lightnings, by portents, and by stars, sometimes by dreams, and sometimes by utterances of persons in a frenzy. And these signs do not often deceive the persons who observe them properly. If prophecies, based on erroneous deductions and interpretations, turn out to be false, the fault is not chargeable to the signs but to the lack of skill in the interpreters.

"Assuming the proposition to be conceded that there is a divine power which pervades the lives of men, it is not hard to understand the principle directing those premonitory signs which we see come to pass. For it may be that the choice of a sacrificial victim is guided by an intelligent force, which is diffused throughout the universe; or, it may be that at the moment when the sacrifice is offered, a change in the vitals occurs and something is added or taken away; for many things are added to, changed, or diminished in an instant of time. ...

liii "The Divine Will accomplishes like results in the case of birds, and causes those known as alites, which give omens by their flight, to fly hither and thither and disappear now here and now there, and causes those known as oscines, which give omens by their cries, to sing now on the left and now on the right. For if every animal moves its body forward, sideways, or backward at will, it bends, twists, extends, and contracts its members as it pleases, and performs these various motions almost mechanically; how much easier it is for such results to be accomplished by a god, whose divine will all things obey! The same power sends us signs, of which history has preserved numerous examples. We find the following omens recorded: when just before sunrise the moon was eclipsed in the sign of Leo, this indicated that Darius and the Persians would be overcome in battle by the Macedonians under Alexander, and that Darius would die. Again, when a girl was born with two heads, this foretold sedition among the people and seduction and adultery in the home. When a woman dreamed that she had been delivered of a lion, this signified that the country in which she had the dream would be conquered by foreign nations.

Purity of Soul Helps Divination

"…Therefore, just as a man has clear and trustworthy dreams, provided he goes to sleep, not only with his mind prepared by noble thoughts, but also with every precaution taken to induce repose; so, too, he, when awake, is better prepared to interpret truly the messages of entrails, stars, birds, and all other signs, provided his soul is pure and undefiled.

liv "It is the purity of soul, no doubt, that explains that famous utterance which history attributes to Socrates and which his disciples in their books often represent him as repeating: 'There is some divine influence' — *daimonion*, he called it — 'which I always obey, though it never urges me on, but often holds me back.' And it was the same Socrates — and what better authority can we quote? — who was consulted by Xenophon as to whether he should join Cyrus. Socrates, after stating what seemed to him the best thing to do, remarked: 'But my opinion is only that of a man. In matters of doubt and perplexity I advise that Apollo's oracle be consulted.' This oracle was always consulted by the Athenians in regard to the more serious public questions.

"It is also related of Socrates that one day he saw his friend Crito with a bandage on his eye. 'What's the matter, Crito?' he inquired. 'As I was walking in the country the branch of a tree, which had been bent, was released and struck me in the eye.' 'Of course,' said Socrates, 'for, after I had had divine warning, as usual, and tried to call you

back, you did not heed.' It is also related of him that after the
unfortunate battle was fought at Delium under command
of Laches, he was fleeing in company with his commander,
when they came to a place where three roads met. Upon his
refusal to take the road that the others had chosen he was
asked the reason and replied: 'The god prevents me.' Those
who fled by the other road fell in with the enemy's cavalry.
Antipater has gathered a mass of remarkable premonitions
received by Socrates, but I shall pass them by, for you know
them and it is useless for me to recount them. However, the
following utterance of that philosopher, made after he had
been wickedly condemned to death, is a noble one—I might
almost call it 'divine': 'I am very content to die,' he said;
'for neither when I left my home nor when I mounted the
platform to plead my cause, did the god give any sign, and
this he always does when some evil threatens me.'

Divination Exists Despite Errors

lv "And so my opinion is that the power of divination
exists, notwithstanding the fact that those who prophesy
by means of art and conjecture are oftentimes mistaken. I
believe that, just as men may make mistakes in other callings,
so they may in this. It may happen that a sign of doubtful
meaning is assumed to be certain or, possibly, either a sign
was itself unobserved or one that annulled an observed
sign may have gone unnoticed. But, in order to establish
the proposition for which I contend it is enough for me to
find, not many, but even a few instances of divinely inspired
prevision and prophecy. Nay, if even one such instance is
found and the agreement between the prediction and the
thing predicted is so close as to exclude every semblance of
chance or of accident, I should not hesitate to say in such a
case, that divination undoubtedly exists and that everybody
should admit its existence.

Posidonius on Divination by Art and Nature

"Wherefore, it seems to me that we must do as Posidonius
does and trace the vital principle of divination in its entirety

to three sources: first, to God, whose connection with the subject has been sufficiently discussed; secondly to Fate; and lastly, to Nature. Reason compels us to admit that all things happen by Fate. Now by Fate I mean the same that the Greeks call *eimarmenê*, that is, an orderly succession of causes wherein cause is linked to cause and each cause of itself produces an effect. That is an immortal truth having its source in all eternity. Therefore nothing has happened which was not bound to happen, and, likewise, nothing is going to happen which will not find in nature every efficient cause of its happening. Consequently, we know that Fate is that which is called, not ignorantly, but scientifically, 'the eternal cause of things, the wherefore of things past, of things present, and of things to come.' Hence it is that it may be known by observation what effect will in most instances follow any cause, even if it is not known in all; for it would be too much to say that it is known in every case. And it is probable that these causes of coming events are perceived by those who see them during frenzy or in sleep.

lvi "Moreover, since, as will be shown elsewhere, all things happen by Fate, if there were a man whose soul could discern the links that join each cause with every other cause, then surely he would never be mistaken in any prediction he might make. For he who knows the causes of future events necessarily knows what every future event will be. But since such knowledge is possible only to a god, it is left to man to presage the future by means of certain signs which indicate what will follow them. Things which are to be do not suddenly spring into existence, but the evolution of time is like the unwinding of a cable: it creates nothing new and only unfolds each event in its order.

"This connection between cause and effect is obvious to two classes of diviners: those who are endowed with natural divination and those who know the course of events by the observation of signs. They may not discern the causes themselves, yet they do discern the signs and tokens of those causes. The careful study and recollection of those signs, aided by the records of former times, has evolved that sort of divination, known as artificial, which is divination by means of entrails, lightnings, portents, and celestial phenomena.

"Therefore it is not strange that diviners have a presentiment of things that exist nowhere in the material world: for all things 'are,' though, from the standpoint of 'time,' they are not present. As in seeds there inheres the germ of those things which the seeds produce, so in causes are stored the future events whose coming is foreseen by reason or conjecture, or is discerned by the soul when inspired by frenzy, or when it is set free by sleep. Persons familiar with the rising, setting, and revolutions of the sun, moon, and other celestial bodies, can tell long in advance where any one of these bodies will be at a given time. And the same thing may be said of men who, for a long period of time, have studied and noted the course of facts and the connection of events, for they always know what the future will be; or, if that is putting it too strongly, they know in a majority of cases; or, if that will not be conceded either, then, surely, they sometimes know what the future will be. These and a few other arguments of the same kind for the existence of divination are derived from Fate.

lvii "Moreover, divination finds another and a positive support in nature, which teaches us how great is the power of the soul when it is divorced from the bodily senses, as it is especially in sleep, and in times of frenzy or inspiration. For, as the souls of the gods, without the intervention of eyes or ears or tongue, understand each other and what each one thinks (hence men, even when they offer silent prayers and vows, have no doubt that the gods understand them), so the souls of men, when released by sleep from bodily chains, or when stirred by inspiration and delivered up to their own impulses, see things that they cannot see when they are mingled with the body.

"And while it is difficult, perhaps, to apply this principle of nature to explain that kind of divination which we call artificial, yet Posidonius, who digs into the question as deep as one can, thinks that nature gives certain signs of future events. Thus Heraclides of Pontus records that it is the custom of the people of Ceos, once each year, to make a careful observation of the rising of the Dog-star and from such observation to conjecture whether the ensuing year will be healthy or pestilential. For if the star rises dim and, as it were enveloped in a fog, this indicates a thick and heavy atmosphere, which will give off very unwholesome vapors; but if the star appears clear and brilliant, this is a sign that the atmosphere is light and pure and, as a consequence, will be conducive to good health.

Digression on Divination by Art

"Again, Democritus expresses the opinion that the ancients acted wisely in providing for the inspection of the entrails of sacrifices; because, as he thinks, the color and general condition of the entrails are prophetic sometimes of health and sometimes of sickness and sometimes also of whether the fields will be barren or productive. Now, if it is known by observation and experience that these means of divination have their source in nature, it must be that the observations made and records kept for a long period of time have added much to our knowledge of this subject.

...

"Since all things have one and the same and that a common home, and since the human soul has always been and will always be, why, then, should it not be able to understand what effect will follow any cause, and what sign will precede any event?

Conclusion to Two Works on Divination
by Cicero
From *De Divinatione* I: lvii-lviii

Introduction

Quintus ends his discourse with a caution saying that he does not recognize false diviners.

Cicero's Conclusion

"This," said Quintus, "is all that I had to say on divination."

lviii "I will assert, however, in conclusion, that I do not recognize fortune-tellers, or those who prophesy for money, or necromancers, or mediums, whom your friend Appius makes it a practice to consult.

...

When Quintus had finished I remarked, "My dear Quintus, you have come admirably well prepared."

Against Astrology
by Panaetius
from *De Divinatione* Book II: xlii-xlvii

Introduction

Cicero's *De Divinatione* is a dialog between Cicero and his brother Quintus. In Book I, Quintus defends divination in using arguments taken mainly from the Stoics, and most of his discourse is included above under the heading "Two Stoic Works on Divination." In Book II, Cicero attacks divination in using arguments taken mainly from the Academic skeptics, and most of his discourse is included in *Philosophy of the Skeptical Academy*. In addition to these skeptical arguments, however, Cicero also includes this work against astrology, where he says (in his conclusion below) that he is "repeating" the arguments of Panaetius the Stoic, rather than the arguments of Carneades the Academic skeptic.

Panaetius of Rhodes, scholarch of the Stoic school from 129 to c. 110/9 BC, was the most eclectic of the Stoics, influenced by Aristotle and Plato and modifying traditional Stoic doctrine by incorporating some of their ideas into his own philosophy.

He was the only major Stoic philosopher who did not believe in divination. Thus, these arguments against astrology are probably part of a larger work by Panaetius against divination generally.

Cicero's Framing

xlii "Let us come to Chaldean manifestations. In discussing them Plato's pupil, Eudoxus, whom the best scholars consider easily the first in astronomy, has left the following opinion in writing: 'No reliance whatever is to be placed in Chaldean astrologers when they profess to forecast a man's future from the position of the stars on the day of his birth.'

Against Astrology

"Panaetius, too, who was the only one of the Stoics to reject the prophecies of astrologers, mentions Anchialus and Cassander as the greatest astronomers of his day and states that they did not employ their art as a means of divining, though they were eminent in all other branches of astronomy. Scylax of Halicarnassus, an intimate friend of Panaetius, and an eminent astronomer, besides being the head of the government in his own city, utterly repudiated the Chaldean method of foretelling the future.

"But let us dismiss our witnesses and employ reasoning. Those men who defend the natal-day prophecies of the Chaldeans, argue in this way: 'In the starry belt which the Greeks call the Zodiac there is a certain force of such a nature that every part of that belt affects and changes the heavens in a different way, according to the stars that are in this or in an adjoining locality at a given time. This force is variously affected by those stars which are called 'planets' or wandering' stars. But when they have come into that sign of the Zodiac under which someone is born, or into a sign having some connection with or accord with the natal sign, they form what is called a 'triangle' or 'square.' Now since, through the procession and retrogression of the stars, the great variety and change of the seasons and of temperature take place, and since the power of the sun produces such results as are before our eyes, they believe that it is not merely probable, but certain, that just as the temperature of the air is regulated by this celestial force, so also children at their birth are influenced in soul and body and by this force their minds, manners, disposition, physical condition, career in life and destinies are determined.

xliii "What inconceivable madness! For it is not enough to call an opinion 'foolishness' when it is utterly devoid of reason. However, Diogenes the Stoic makes some concessions to the Chaldeans. He says that they have the power of prophecy to the extent of being able to tell the disposition of any child and the calling for which he is best fitted. All their other claims of prophetic powers he absolutely denies. He says, for example, that twins are alike in appearance, but that they generally unlike in career and in fortune. Procles and Eurysthenes, kings of the Lacedaemonians, were twin brothers. 91 But they did not live the same number of years, for the life of Procles was shorter by a year than that of his brother and his deeds were far more glorious. But for my part I say that even this concession which our excellent friend Diogenes makes to the Chaldeans in a sort of collusive way is in itself unintelligible. For the Chaldeans, according to their own statements, believe that a person's destiny is affected by the condition of the moon at the time of his birth, and hence they make and record their observations of the stars which anything in conjunction with the moon on his birthday. As a result, in forming their judgments, they depend on the sense of sight, which is the least trustworthy of the senses, whereas they should employ reason and intelligence. For the science of mathematics which the Chaldeans ought to know, teaches us how close the moon comes to the earth, which indeed it almost touches; how far it is from Mercury, the nearest star; how much further yet it is from Venus; and what a great interval separates it from the sun, which is supposed to give it light. The three remaining distances are beyond computation: from the Sun to Mars, from Mars to Jupiter, from Jupiter to Saturn. Then there is the distance from Saturn to the limits of heaven — the ultimate bounds of space. In view, therefore, of these almost limitless distances, what influence can the planets exercise upon the moon, or rather, upon the earth?

xliv "Again, when the Chaldeans say, as they are bound to do, that all persons born anywhere in the habitable earth under the same horoscope, are alike and must have the same fate, is it not evident that these would-be interpreters of the sky are of a class who are utterly ignorant of the nature of the sky? For the earth is, as it were, divided in half and our view limited by those circles which the Greeks call *horizontes*, and which we may in all accuracy term *finientes* or horizons. Now these horizons vary without limit according to the position of the spectator. Hence, of necessity, the rising and setting of the stars will not occur at the same time for all persons. But if this stellar force affects the heavens now in one way and now in another, how is it possible for this force to operate alike on all persons who are born at the same time, in view of the fact that they are born under vastly different skies? In those places in which we live the Dog-star rises after the solstice, in fact, several days later. But among the Troglodytes, we read, it sets before the solstice. Hence if we should now admit that some stellar influence affects persons who are born upon the earth, then it must be conceded that all persons born at the same time may have different natures owing to the differences in their horoscopes. This is a conclusion by no means agreeable to the astrologers; for they insist that all persons born at the same time, regardless of the place of birth, are born to the same fate.

xlv "But what utter madness in these astrologers, in considering the effect of the vast movements and changes in the heavens, to assume that wind and rain and weather anywhere have no effect at birth! In neighboring places conditions in these respects are so different that frequently, for instance, we have one state of weather at Tusculum and another at Rome. This is especially noticeable to mariners who often observe extreme changes of weather take place while they rounding the capes. Therefore, in view of the fact that the heavens are now serene and now disturbed by storms, is it the part of a reasonable man to say that this fact has no natal influence—and of course it has not—and then assert that a natal influence is exerted by some subtle, imperceptible, well-nigh inconceivable force which is due to the condition of the sky, which condition, in turn, is due to the action of the moon and stars?

"Again, is it no small error of judgment that the Chaldeans fail to realize the effect of the parental seed which is an essential element of the process of generation? For, surely, no one fails to see that the appearance and habits, and generally, the carriage and gestures of children are derived from their parents. This would not be the case if the characteristics of children were determined, not by the natural power of heredity, but by the phases of the moon and by the condition of the sky. And, again, the fact that men who were born at the very same instant, are unlike in character, career, and in destiny, makes it very clear that the time of birth has nothing to do in determining man's course in life. …

xlvi "Furthermore, is it not a well-known and undoubted fact that many persons who were born with certain natural defects have been restored completely by Nature herself, after she had resumed her sway, or by surgery or by medicine? For example, some, who were so tongue-tied that they could not speak, have had their tongues set free by a cut from the surgeon's knife. Many more have corrected a natural defect by intelligent exertion. Demosthenes is an instance: according to the account given by Phalereus, he was unable to pronounce the Greek letter rho, but by repeated effort learned to articulate it perfectly. But if such defects had been engendered and implanted by a star nothing could have changed them. Do not unlike places produce unlike men? It would be an easy matter to sketch rapidly in passing the differences in mind and body which distinguish the Indians from the Persians and the Ethiopians from the Syrians " differences so striking and so pronounced as to be incredible. Hence it is evident that one's birth is more affected by local environment than by the condition of the moon. Of course, the statement quoted by you that the Babylonians for 470,000 years had taken the horoscope of every child and had tested it by the results, is untrue; for if this had been their habit they would not have abandoned it.

Moreover we find no writer who says that the practice exists or who knows that it ever did exist.

Cicero's Conclusion

xlvii "You observe that I am not repeating the arguments of Carneades [the Academic skeptic], but those of Panaetius, the head of the Stoic school. But now on my own initiative I put the following questions: Did all the Romans who fell at Cannae have the same horoscope? Yet all had one and the same end. Were all the men eminent for intellect and genius born under the same star? Was there ever a day when countless numbers were not born? And yet there never was another Homer. Again: if it matters under what aspect of the sky or combination of the stars every animate being is born, then necessarily the same conditions must affect inanimate beings also: can any statement be more ridiculous than that? ..."

On Politics
by Panaetius and Cicero
from *Republica* I: xx-xxxvi and xliv-xlvi

Introduction

Scipio Africanus (236–183 BC) was a Roman consul and general, who gathered a circle of intellectuals around him that included the Stoic philosopher Panaetius and the Roman historian Polybius. In Cicero's *De Republica*, the other speakers ask Scipio to discourse on the subject of politics, because he had many conversations with Panaetius and Polybius, and because he is a master of the arguments proving that the Roman state is the best form of government. These two thinkers from his group are clearly the source of the ideas in Scipio's discourse.

Panaetius was the most eclectic of the Stoic philosophers, combining ideas from other philosophers with traditional Stoic ideas. For example, he believed Aristotle's doctrine that the universe has always existed, rather than the usual Stoic doctrine that the universe is periodically destroyed. Judging from this selection, his political thinking is also based on Aristotle, whose *Politics* says that there are three structures of government, monarchy, aristocracy, and democracy, and that each can exist in either a benevolent or destructive form, as Panaetius says here. Here, the theory has an Stoic twist in the claim that monarchy is the best of the three, because it resembles the entire universe, which is (according to the Stoics) governed by one mind — though it also says that a mixed system with elements of all three is better than any of the three alone, which is inconsistent with the Stoic view of the universe.

The conclusion at the end of the discourse is a transition

to Scipio's discussion of the constitution of Rome as the best form of government, which clearly is based on Polybius rather than on Panaetius.

Zeno of Citium, the founder of Stoicism, also wrote a book named *Republic* (*Politeia* in Greek) describing a utopian Stoic society, which survives only in references in later works. Plutarch summarizes this book:

> the much-admired *Republic* of Zeno, the founder of the Stoic sect, may be summed up in this one main principle: that all the inhabitants of this world of ours should not live differentiated by their respective rules of justice into separate cities and communities, but that we should consider all men to be of one community and one polity, and that we should have a common life and an order common to us all, even as a herd that feeds together and shares the pasturage of a common field. This Zeno wrote, giving shape to a dream or, as it were, shadowy picture of a well-ordered and philosophic commonwealth....[42]

Diogenes Laertius, summarizing the books most controversial points, says:

> ... in the *Republic* ... he [Zeno] declares the good alone to be true citizens or friends or kindred or free men; and accordingly in the view of the Stoics parents and children are enemies, not being wise. Again, it is objected, in the *Republic* he lays down community of wives, and at line 200 prohibits the building of temples, law-courts and gymnasia in cities; while as regards a currency he writes that we should not think it need be introduced either for purposes of exchange or for traveling abroad. Further, he bids men and women wear the same dress and keep no part of the body entirely covered.[43]

42   Plutarch, "On the Fortune or the Virtue of Alexander the Great" 6: 1 from Plutarch, *Moralia*, translated by Frank Cole Babbitt (Cambridge, Harvard University Press, 1936) vol. iv, p. 398.

43   Diogenes Laertius, vii: 33 Diogenes Laertius, *Lives of Eminent*

Chrysippus, the greatest Stoic philosopher, wrote a *Republic* that defended incest,[44] and he may have been responding to criticisms that Zeno's community of women would inevitably lead to incest, since people would not know who had the same father.

Obviously, the Stoics' ideas about politics became much more respectable under Panaetius. It is a great loss that we do not have more of these earlier works about politics, which represented purer Stoic thinking than Panaetius' ideas, based largely on Aristotle.

Cicero wrote an earlier *De Republica* when he held offices in the Roman government. This discussion supposedly occurred before Cicero's birth, and Cicero says he heard an account of it when he was young. Yet the speakers sometimes cite Cicero's ideas about government, copied from the earlier *De Republica*, though Cicero was not yet born when Scipio died. These citations make it clear that Cicero added his own ideas to Panaetius' in the later *De Republica*, and we omit the direct citations from Cicero to come closer to the ideas of Panaetius.

Cicero wrote his brother Quintus saying that writing the later *De Republica* was slow and difficult work, [45] not just a matter of transcribing Greek ideas in Latin like many of his philosophical dialogs. Thus, it seems likely that he did much more reworking of his sources here than in most of his dialogs, which is why we list both Panaetius and Cicero as the authors of this work.

Cicero's Framing

xx Then Mucius said: "What, then, do you consider, my Laelius, should be our best arguments in endeavoring to bring about the object of your wishes?"

Laelius: "Those sciences and arts which teach us how we may be most useful to the State; for I consider that the most

---

Philosophers, translated by R.D. Hicks (Cambridge, Harvard University Press: Loeb Classical Library, 1925) p. 145.

44 Diogenes Laertius, vii: 188.

45 Cicero, *Epistulae Ad Quintum Fratrem*: II, 12.

glorious office of wisdom, and the noblest proof and business of virtue. In order, therefore, that we may consecrate these holidays as much as possible to conversations which may be profitable to the Commonwealth, let us beg Scipio to explain to us what in his estimation appears to be the best form of government. Then let us pass on to other points, the knowledge of which may lead us, as I hope, to sound political views, and unfold the causes of the dangers which now threaten us."

xxi When Philus, Manilius, and Mummius had all expressed their great approbation of this idea [gap in the text] "I have ventured [to open our discussion] in this way, not only because it is but just that on State politics the chief man in the State should be the principal speaker, but also because I recollect that you, Scipio, were formerly very much in the habit of conversing with Panaetius and Polybius, two Greeks, exceedingly learned in political questions, and that you are master of many arguments by which you prove that by far the best condition of government is that which our ancestors have handed down to us. And as you, therefore, are familiar with this subject, if you will explain to us your views respecting the general principles of a state (I speak for my friends as well as myself), we shall feel exceedingly obliged to you."

xxii Then Scipio said: "I must acknowledge that there is no subject of meditation to which my mind naturally turns with more ardor and intensity than this very one which Laelius has proposed to us. And, indeed, as I see that in every profession, every artist who would distinguish himself, thinks of, and aims at, and labors for no other object but that of attaining perfection in his art, should not I, whose main business, according to the example of my father and my ancestors, is the advancement and right administration of government, be confessing myself more indolent than any common mechanic if I were to bestow on this noblest of sciences less attention and labor than they devote to their insignificant trades?

...

xxiv Then Scipio proceeded: "I will do what you wish, as far as I can; and I shall enter into the discussion under favor of that rule which, I think, should be adopted by all persons in disputations of this kind, if they wish to avoid being misunderstood; namely, that when men have agreed respecting the proper name of the matter under discussion, it should be stated what that name exactly means, and what it legitimately includes. And when that point is settled, then it is fit to enter on the discussion; for it will never be possible to arrive at an understanding of what the character of the subject of the discussion is, unless one first understands exactly what it is. Since, then, our investigations relate to a commonwealth, we must first examine what this name properly signifies."

And when Laelius had intimated his approbation of this course, Scipio continued:

"I shall not adopt, said he, in so clear and simple a manner that system of discussion which goes back to first principles; as learned men often do in this sort of discussion, so as to go back to the first meeting of male and female, and then to the first birth and formation of the first family, and define over and over again what there is in words, and in how many manners each thing is stated. For, as I am speaking to men of prudence, who have acted with the greatest glory in the Commonwealth, both in peace and war, I will take care not to allow the subject of the discussion itself to be clearer than my explanation of it. Nor have I undertaken this task with the design of examining all its minuter points, like a schoolmaster; nor will I promise you in the following discourse not to omit any single particular."

Then Laelius said: "For my part, I am impatient for exactly that kind of disquisition which you promise us."

Origin and Types of Commonwealths

xxv "Well, then," said Africanus, "a commonwealth is a constitution of the entire people. But the people is not every association of men, however congregated, but the association of the entire number, bound together by the compact of justice, and the communication of utility. The first cause of this association is not so much the weakness of man as a certain spirit of congregation which naturally belongs to him. For the human race is not a race of isolated individuals, wandering and solitary; but it is so constituted that even in the affluence of all things [and without any need of reciprocal assistance, it spontaneously seeks society].

[about fifteen lines of the manuscript are lost]

xxvi "[It is necessary to presuppose] these original seeds, as it were, since we cannot discover any primary establishment of the other virtues, or even of a commonwealth itself. These unions, then, formed by the principle which I have mentioned, established their headquarters originally in certain central positions, for the convenience of the whole population; and having fortified them by natural and artificial means, they called this collection of houses a city or town, distinguished by temples and public squares. Every people, therefore, which consists of such an association of the entire multitude as I have described, every city which consists of an assemblage of the people, and every commonwealth which embraces every member of these associations, must be regulated by a certain authority, in order to be permanent.

"This intelligent authority should always refer itself to that grand first principle which established the Commonwealth. It must be deposited in the hands of one supreme person, or entrusted to the administration of certain delegated rulers, or undertaken by the whole multitude. When the direction of all depends on one person, we call this individual a king, and this form of political constitution a kingdom. When it is in the power of privileged delegates, the State is said to be ruled by an aristocracy; and when the people are all in all, they call it a democracy, or popular constitution. And if the tie of social affection, which originally united men in political associations for the sake of public interest, maintains its force, each of these forms of government is, I will not say perfect, nor, in my opinion, essentially good, but tolerable, and such that one may accidentally be better than another: either a just and wise king, or a selection of the most eminent citizens, or even the populace itself (though this is the least commendable form), may, if there be no interference of crime and cupidity, form a constitution sufficiently secure.

xxvii "But in a monarchy the other members of the State are often too much deprived of public counsel and jurisdiction; and under the rule of an aristocracy the multitude can hardly possess its due share of liberty, since it is allowed no share in the public deliberation, and no power. And when all things are carried by a democracy, although it be just and moderate, yet its very equality is a culpable leveling, inasmuch as it allows no gradations of rank. Therefore, even if Cyrus, the King of the Persians, was a most righteous and wise monarch, I should still think that the interest of the people (for this is, as I have said before, the same as the Commonwealth) could not be very effectually promoted when all things depended on the beck and nod of one individual. And though at present the people of Marseilles, our clients, are governed with the greatest justice by elected magistrates of the highest rank, still there is always in this condition of the people a certain appearance of servitude; and when the Athenians, at a certain period, having demolished their Areopagus, conducted all public affairs by the acts and decrees of the democracy alone, their State, as it no longer contained a distinct gradation of ranks, was no longer able to retain its original fair appearance.

xxviii "I have reasoned thus on the three forms of government, not looking on them in their disorganized and confused conditions, but in their proper and regular administration. These three particular forms, however, contained in themselves, from the first, the faults and defects I have mentioned; but they have also other dangerous vices, for there is not one of these three forms of government which has not a precipitous and slippery passage down to some proximate abuse. For, after thinking of that endurable, or, as you will have it, most amiable king, Cyrus—to name him in preference to any one else—then, to produce a change in our minds, we behold the barbarous Phalaris, that model of tyranny, to which the monarchical authority is easily abused by a facile and natural inclination. And, in like manner, along-side of the wise aristocracy of Marseilles, we might exhibit the oligarchical faction of the thirty tyrants which once existed at Athens. And, not to seek for other instances, among the same Athenians, we can show you that when unlimited power was cast into the hands of the people, it inflamed the fury of the multitude, and aggravated that universal license which ruined their State. [a gap in the text]

xxix "The worst condition of things sometimes results from a confusion of those factious tyrannies into which kings, aristocrats, and democrats are apt to degenerate. For thus, from these diverse elements, there occasionally arises (as I have said before) a new kind of government. And wonderful indeed are the revolutions and periodical returns in natural constitutions of such alternations and vicissitudes, which it is the part of the wise politician to investigate with the closest attention. But to calculate their approach, and to join to this foresight the skill which moderates the course of events, and retains in a steady hand the reins of that authority which safely conducts the people through all the dangers to which they expose themselves, is the work of a most illustrious citizen, and of almost divine genius.

"There is a fourth kind of government, therefore, which, in my opinion, is preferable to all these: it is that mixed and moderate government which is composed of the three particular forms which I have already noticed.

xxx Laelius: "I am not ignorant, Scipio, that such is your opinion, for I have often heard you say so. But I do not the less desire, if it is not giving you too much trouble, to hear which you consider the best of these three forms of commonwealths. For it may be of some use in considering [gap in the text]"

Arguments for Democracy

xxxi [gap in the text] "And each commonwealth corresponds to the nature and will of him who governs it. Therefore, in no other constitution than that in which the people exercise sovereign power has liberty any sure abode, than which there certainly is no more desirable blessing. And if it be not equally established for every one, it is not even liberty at all. And how can there be this character of equality, I do not say under a monarchy, where slavery is least disguised or doubtful, but even in those constitutions in which the people are free indeed in words, for they give their suffrages, they elect officers, they are canvassed and solicited for magistracies; but yet they only grant those things which they are obliged to grant whether they will or not, and which are not really in their free power, though others ask them for them? For they are not themselves admitted to the government, to the exercise of public authority, or to offices of select judges, which are permitted to those only of ancient families and large fortunes. But in a free people, as among the Rhodians and Athenians, there is no citizen who [gap in the text]

xxxii [gap in the text] "No sooner is one man, or several, elevated by wealth and power, than they say that [gap in the text] arise from their pride and arrogance, when the idle and the timid give way, and bow down to the insolence of riches. But if the people knew how to maintain its rights, then they say that nothing could be more glorious and prosperous than democracy; inasmuch as they themselves would be the sovereign dispensers of laws, judgments, war, peace, public treaties, and, finally, of the fortune and life of each individual citizen; and this condition of things is the only one which, in their opinion, can be really called a commonwealth, that is to say, a constitution of the people. It is on this principle that, according to them, a people often vindicates its liberty from the domination of kings and nobles; while, on the other hand, kings are not sought for among free peoples, nor are the power and wealth of aristocracies. They deny, moreover, that it is fair to reject this general constitution of freemen, on account of the vices of the unbridled populace; but that if the people be united and inclined, and directs all its efforts to the safety and freedom of the community, nothing can be stronger or more unchangeable; and they assert that this necessary union is easily obtained in a republic so constituted that the good of all classes is the same; while the conflicting interests that prevail in other constitutions inevitably produce dissensions; therefore, say they, when the senate had the ascendency, the republic had no stability; and when kings possess the power, this blessing is still more rare, since, as Ennius expresses it,

In kingdoms there's no faith, and little love.

Wherefore, since the law is the bond of civil society, and the justice of the law equal, by what rule can the association of citizens be held together, if the condition of the citizens be not equal? For if the fortunes of men cannot be reduced to this equality — if genius cannot be equally the property of all — rights, at least, should be equal among those who are citizens of the same republic. For what is a republic but an association of rights? [gap in the text]

xxxiii But as to the other political constitutions, these democratical advocates do not think they are worthy of being distinguished by the name which they claim. For why, say they, should we apply the name of king, the title of Jupiter the Beneficent, and not rather the title of tyrant, to a man ambitious of sole authority and power, lording it over a degraded multitude? For a tyrant may be as merciful as a king may be oppressive; so that the whole difference to the people is, whether they serve an indulgent master or a cruel one, since serve some one they must. But how could Sparta, at the period of the boasted superiority of her political institution, obtain a constant enjoyment of just and virtuous kings, when they necessarily received an hereditary monarch, good, bad, or indifferent, because he happened to be of the blood royal? As to aristocrats, Who will endure, say they, that men should distinguish themselves by such a title, and that not by the voice of the people, but by their own votes? For how is such a one judged to be best either in learning, sciences, or arts? [gap in the text]

Arguments for Aristocracy

xxxiv [gap in the text] "If it does so by hap-hazard, it will be as easily upset as a vessel if the pilot were chosen by lot from among the passengers. But if a people, being free, chooses those to whom it can trust itself — and, if it desires its own preservation, it will always choose the noblest — then certainly it is in the counsels of the aristocracy that the safety of the State consists, especially as nature has not only appointed that these superior men should excel the inferior sort in high virtue and courage, but has inspired the people also with the desire of obedience towards these, their natural lords. But they say this aristocratical State is destroyed by the depraved opinions of men, who, through ignorance of virtue (which, as it belongs to few, can be discerned and appreciated by few), imagine that not only rich and powerful men, but also those who are nobly born, are necessarily the best. And so when, through this popular error, the riches, and not the virtue, of a few men has taken possession of the State, these chiefs obstinately retain the title of nobles, though they want the essence of nobility. For riches, fame, and power, without wisdom and a just method of regulating ourselves and commanding others, are full of discredit and insolent arrogance; nor is there any kind of government more deformed than that in which the wealthiest are regarded as the noblest.

"But when virtue governs the Commonwealth, what can be more glorious? When he who commands the rest is himself enslaved by no lust or passion; when he himself exhibits all the virtues to which he incites and educates the citizens; when he imposes no law on the people which he does not himself observe, but presents his life as a living law to his fellow-countrymen; if a single individual could thus suffice for all, there would be no need of more; and if the community could find a chief ruler thus worthy of all their suffrages, none would require elected magistrates.

"It was the difficulty of forming plans which transferred the government from a king into the hands of many; and the error and temerity of the people likewise transferred it from the hands of the many into those of the few. Thus, between the weakness of the monarch and the rashness of the multitude, the aristocrats have occupied the middle place, than which nothing can be better arranged; and while they superintend the public interest, the people necessarily enjoy the greatest possible prosperity, being free from all care and anxiety, having entrusted their security to others, who ought sedulously to defend it, and not allow the people to suspect that their advantage is neglected by their rulers.

"For as to that equality of rights which democracies so loudly boast of, it can never be maintained; for the people themselves, so dissolute and so unbridled, are always inclined to flatter a number of demagogues; and there is in them a very great partiality for certain men and dignities, so that their equality, so called, becomes most unfair and iniquitous. For as equal honor is given to the most noble and the most infamous, some of whom must exist in every State, then the equity which they eulogize becomes most inequitable — an evil which never can happen in those states which are governed by aristocracies. These reasonings, my Laelius, and some others of the same kind, are usually brought forward by those that so highly extol this form of political constitution."

Monarchy Is the Best of the Three

xxxv Then Laelius said: "But you have not told us, Scipio, which of these three forms of government you yourself most approve."

Scipio: "You are right to shape your question, which of the three I most approve, for there is not one of them which I approve at all by itself, since, as I told you, I prefer that government which is mixed and composed of all these

forms, to any one of them taken separately. But if I must
confine myself to one of these particular forms simply and
exclusively, I must confess I prefer the royal one, and praise
that as the first and best. In this, which I here choose to call
the primitive form of government, I find the title of father
attached to that of king, to express that he watches over
the citizens as over his children, and endeavors rather to
preserve them in freedom than reduce them to slavery. So
that it is more advantageous for those who are insignificant
in property and capacity to be supported by the care of one
excellent and eminently powerful man. The nobles here
present themselves, who profess that they can do all this
in much better style; for they say that there is much more
wisdom in many than in one, and at least as much faith and
equity. And, last of all, come the people, who cry with a
loud voice that they will render obedience neither to the one
nor the few; that even to brute beasts nothing is so dear as
liberty; and that all men who serve either kings or nobles
are deprived of it. Thus, the kings attract us by affection, the
nobles by talent, the people by liberty; and in the comparison
it is hard to choose the best."

Laelius: "I think so too, but yet it is impossible to dispatch
the other branches of the question, if you leave this primary
point undetermined."

xxxvi Scipio: "We must then, I suppose, imitate Aratus,
who, when he prepared himself to treat of great things,
thought himself in duty bound to begin with Jupiter."

Laelius: "Wherefore Jupiter? and what is there in this
discussion which resembles that poem?"

Scipio. "Why, it serves to teach us that we cannot better
commence our investigations than by invoking him whom,
with one voice, both learned and unlearned extol as the
universal king of all gods and men."

"How so?" said Laelius.

"Do you, then," asked Scipio, "believe in nothing
which is not before your eyes? whether these ideas have
been established by the chiefs of states for the benefit of
society, that there might be believed to exist one Universal

Monarch in heaven, at whose nod (as Homer expresses it) all Olympus trembles, and that he might be accounted both king and father of all creatures; for there is great authority, and there are many witnesses, if you choose to call all many, who attest that all nations have unanimously recognized, by the decrees of their chiefs, that nothing is better than a king, since they think that all the Gods are governed by the divine power of one sovereign; or if we suspect that this opinion rests on the error of the ignorant, and should be classed among the fables, let us listen to those universal testimonies of erudite men, who have, as it were, seen with their eyes those things to the knowledge of which we can hardly attain by report."

"What men do you mean?" said Laelius.

"Those," replied Scipio, "who, by the investigation of nature, have arrived at the opinion that the whole universe [is animated] by a single Mind." [gap in the text]

[Here there is a long series of historical examples, with much back-and-forth between Laelius and Scipio, which seems to be Cicero's addition.]

The Mixed Constitution

xliv Scipio: Now, to return to the argument of my discourse. It appears that this extreme license, which is the only liberty in the eyes of the vulgar, is, according to Plato, such that from it as a sort of root tyrants naturally arise and spring up. For as the excessive power of an aristocracy occasions the destruction of the nobles, so this excessive liberalism of democracies brings after it the slavery of the people. Thus we find in the weather, the soil, and the animal constitution the most favorable conditions are sometimes suddenly converted by their excess into the contrary, and this fact is especially observable in political governments; and this excessive liberty soon brings the people collectively and individually to an excessive servitude. For, as I said, this extreme liberty easily introduces the reign of tyranny, the severest of all unjust slaveries. In fact, from the midst of this unbridled and capricious populace, they elect someone as a leader in opposition to their afflicted and expelled nobles: some new chief, forsooth, audacious and impure, often insolently persecuting those who have deserved well of the State, and ready to gratify the populace at his neighbor's expense as well as his own. Then, since the private condition is naturally exposed to fears and alarms, the people invest him with many powers, and these are continued in his hands. Such men, like Pisistratus of Athens, will soon find an excuse for surrounding themselves with body-guards, and they will conclude by becoming tyrants over the very persons who raised them to dignity. If such despots perish by the vengeance of the better citizens, as is generally the case, the constitution is re-established; but if they fall by the hands of bold insurgents, then the same faction succeeds them, which is only another species of tyranny. And the same revolution arises from the fair system of aristocracy when any corruption has betrayed the nobles from the path of rectitude. Thus the power is like the ball which is flung from hand to hand: it passes from kings to tyrants, from tyrants to the aristocracy, from them to democracy, and from these back again to tyrants and to factions; and thus the same kind of government is seldom long maintained.

xlv Since these are the facts of experience, royalty is, in my opinion, very far preferable to the three other kinds of political constitutions. But it is itself inferior to that which is composed of an equal mixture of the three best forms of government, united and modified by one another. I wish to establish in a commonwealth a royal and pre-eminent chief. Another portion of power should be deposited in the hands of the aristocracy, and certain things should be reserved to the judgment and wish of the multitude.

This constitution, in the first place, possesses that great equality without which men cannot long maintain their freedom; secondly, it offers a great stability, while the particular separate and isolated forms easily fall into their contraries; so that a king is succeeded by a despot, an aristocracy by a faction, a democracy by a mob and confusion; and all these forms are frequently sacrificed to new revolutions. In this united and mixed constitution, however, similar disasters cannot happen without the greatest vices in public men. For there can be little to occasion revolution in a state in which every person is firmly established in his appropriate rank, and there are but few modes of corruption into which we can fall.

Cicero's Conclusion

xlvi "But I fear, Laelius, and you, my amiable and learned friends, that if I were to dwell any longer on this argument, my words would seem rather like the lessons of a master, and not like the free conversation of one who is uniting with you in the consideration of truth. I shall therefore pass on to those things which are familiar to all, and which I have long studied. And in these matters I believe, I feel, and I affirm that of all governments there is none which, either in its entire constitution or the distribution of its parts, or in the discipline of its manners, is comparable to that which our fathers received from our earliest ancestors, and which they have handed down to us. And since you wish to hear from me a development of this constitution, with which you are all acquainted, I shall endeavor to explain its true character and excellence. Thus keeping my eye fixed on the model of our Roman Commonwealth, I shall endeavor to accommodate to it all that I have to say on the best form of government. And by treating the subject in this way, I think I shall be able to accomplish most satisfactorily the task which Laelius has imposed on me."

On Duties
by Cicero following Panaetius
from *De Officiis* III: ii-iv

Introduction

Cicero's *De Officiis* (*On Duties*) was based on an unfinished work by Panaetius.

Panaetius' *Peri tou Kathêkontos* (*On Duties*) was meant to contain three parts: the first about how we should act in keeping with our moral duties, the second about how we should act to pursue our advantage, and the third about how we should act when there is a conflict between our moral duties and our advantage. Panaetius wrote the first two parts, but he never wrote the third, though he lived for thirty years after completing the first two. Posidonius wrote a brief sketch of what the third part might say, claiming that "there is no other topic in the whole range of philosophy so essentially important as this."[46]

Cicero rewrote Panaetius' first two parts as the first two books of *De Officiis*, paraphrasing Panaetius, occasionally disagreeing with him, and adding new material. Book I begins with a brief statement of Stoic theory that virtue aims at natural advantages and a description of the cardinal virtues, but most of it is about specific conduct in everyday life that supposedly depends on this theory. Book II gives many examples of how to pursue your personal advantage and be successful, for example how get people to support you by winning their friendship or winning their admiration. Book III gives arguments and examples supporting the obvious Stoic conclusion that only virtuous action is truly to your advantage.

46 *De Officiis* III: ii.

The interesting question in the history of philosophy is how Panaetius could have written this book—and how the Stoics could have considered it so important. We have seen that Stoics believed that virtue is the only good and that it is a matter of indifference whether you achieve the natural advantages that are the aims of the virtues. Why should this book have so much practical advice about how to pursue your personal advantage successfully? And how can it even wonder what you should do when there are conflicts between virtue and personal advantage?

The reason is that Panaetius changed Stoicism and created what we call the "middle Stoa." The early Stoa believed that anything less than perfection was worthless: you were either a wise man who lived according to Stoic doctrines and morality, or you were a failure. The middle Stoa aimed its teaching at ordinary people as well as at prospective wise men, offering maxims that let people act a bit more wisely even though they were not perfect wise men. This book by Panaetius was considered important because it marked this shift in Stoic teaching.

We are not going to try to reconstruct the source text by Panaetius based on Cicero's book. In his dialogs, Cicero has different speakers state the theories of different philosophical schools, and he often takes their speeches directly from source works by these schools. By contrast, *De Officiis* is presented as a series of letters to his son Marcus rather than a dialog, and he clearly is rewriting Panaetius' source document rather than quoting it, as he himself says:

> Panaetius … whom I am following, not slavishly translating, in these books.[47]

All of *De Officiis* is a unified whole, including the two books based on Panaetius and the book that is written entirely by Cicero. It is not patched together like some discourses in the dialogs.

The ideas from Panaetius in *De Officiis* are also too lengthy to excerpt in this book. *De Officiis* is readily available to

---

47 *De Officiis* II: xvii.

anyone who wants to study Panaetius. Cicero states where he is following Panaetius and where he is adding his own thoughts, so it is easy to get a general idea of what Panaetius wrote from Cicero's book, even though it is a rewrite.

Instead of trying to pull the ideas of Panaetius out of *De Officiis*, we will include a brief excerpt where Cicero explains that Panaetius aimed the maxims in this book at ordinary people rather than at the wise man. Cicero attributes these ideas to "the Stoics," but the reader should bear in mind that he is talking about the Stoics of his own time, the middle Stoa. The excerpt is interesting because it shows clearly how different the middle Stoa was from the early Stoa.

Excerpt from *De Officiis* Book III

ii Let us now return to the remaining section of our subject as outlined. Panaetius, then, has given us what is unquestionably the most thorough discussion of moral duties that we have, and I have followed him in the main—but with slight modifications. He classifies under three general heads the ethical problems which people are accustomed to consider and weigh: first, the question whether the matter in hand is morally right or morally wrong; second, whether it is expedient or inexpedient; third, how a decision ought to be reached, in case that which has the appearance of being morally right clashes with that which seems to be expedient. He has treated the first two heads at length in three books; but, while he has stated that he meant to discuss the third head in its proper turn, he has never fulfilled his promise. And I wonder the more at this, because Posidonius, a pupil of his, records that Panaetius was still alive thirty years after he published those three books. And I am surprised that Posidonius has but briefly touched upon this subject in certain memoirs of his, and especially, as he states that there is no other topic in the whole range of philosophy so essentially important as this.

Now, I cannot possibly accept the view of those who say that that point was not overlooked but purposely omitted by Panaetius, and that it was not one that ever needed discussion, because there never can be such a thing as a conflict between expediency and moral rectitude. But with regard to this assertion, the one point may admit of doubt — whether that question which is third in but the other point is not open to debate — that it was included in Panaetius' plan but left unwritten. For, if a writer has finished two divisions of a threefold subject, the third must necessarily remain for him to do. Besides, he promises at the close of the third book that he will discuss this division also in its proper turn. We have also in Posidonius a competent witness to the fact. He writes in one of his letters that Publius Rutilius Rufus, who also was a pupil of Panaetius, used to say that "as no painter had been found to complete that part of the Venus of Cos which Apelles had left unfinished (for the beauty of her face made hopeless any attempt adequately to represent the rest of the figure), so no one, because of the surpassing excellence of what Panaetius did complete, would venture to supply what he had left undone."

iii In regard to Panaetius' real intentions, therefore, no doubt can be entertained. But whether he was or was not justified in adding this third division to the inquiry about duty may, perhaps, be a matter for debate. For whether moral goodness is the only good, as the Stoics believe, or whether, as your Peripatetics think, moral goodness is in so far the highest good that everything else gathered together into the opposing scale would have scarcely the slightest weight, it is beyond question that expediency can never conflict with moral rectitude. And so, we have heard, Socrates used to pronounce a curse upon those who first drew a conceptual distinction between things naturally inseparable. With this doctrine the Stoics are in agreement in so far as they maintain that if anything is morally right, it is expedient, and if anything is not morally right, it is not expedient.

But if Panaetius were the sort of man to say that virtue is worth cultivating only because it is productive of advantage, as do certain philosophers who measure the desirableness of things by the standard of pleasure or of absence of pain [the Epicureans], he might argue that expediency sometimes clashes with moral rectitude. But since he is a man who judges that the morally right is the only good, and that those things which come in conflict with it have only the appearance of expediency and cannot make life any better by their presence nor any worse by their absence, it follows that he ought not to have raised a question involving the weighing of what seems expedient against what is morally right.

Furthermore, when the Stoics speak of the supreme good as "living conformably to Nature," they mean, as I take it, something like this: that we are always to be in accord with virtue, and from all other things that may be in harmony with Nature to choose only such as are not incompatible with virtue. This being so, some people are of the opinion that it was not right to introduce this counterbalancing of right and expediency and that no practical instruction should have been given on this question at all. And yet moral goodness, in the true and proper sense of the term, is the exclusive possession of the wise and can never be separated from virtue; but those who have not perfect wisdom cannot possibly have perfect moral goodness, but only a semblance of it.

And indeed these duties under discussion in these books the Stoics call "mean duties" [that is, "middle duties"]; they are a common possession and have wide application; and many people attain to the knowledge of them through natural goodness of heart and through advancement in learning. But that duty which those same Stoics call "right" is perfect and absolute and "satisfies all the numbers," as that same school says, and is {15} attainable by none except the wise man.

On the other hand, when some act is performed in which we see "mean" duties manifested, that is generally regarded as fully perfect, for the reason that the common crowd does not, as a rule, comprehend how far it falls short of real perfection; but, as far as their comprehension does go, they think there is no deficiency. This same thing ordinarily occurs in the estimation of poems, paintings, and a great many other works of art: ordinary people enjoy and praise things that do not deserve praise. The reason for this, I suppose, is that those productions have some point of excellence which catches the fancy of the uneducated, because these have not the ability to discover the points of weakness in any particular piece of work before them. And so, when they are instructed by experts, they readily abandon their former opinion.

iv The performance of the duties, then, which I am discussing in these books, is called by the Stoics a sort of second-grade moral goodness, not the peculiar property of their wise men, but shared by them with all mankind. Accordingly, such duties appeal to all men who have a natural disposition to virtue. And when the two Decii or the two Scipios are mentioned as "brave men" or Fabricius is called "the just," it is not at all that the former are quoted as perfect models of courage or the latter as a perfect model of justice, as if we had in one of them the ideal "wise man." For no one of them was wise in the sense in which we wish to have "wise" understood; neither were Marcus Cato and Gaius Laelius wise, though they were so considered and were surnamed "the wise." Not even the famous Seven were "wise." But because of their constant observance of "mean" duties they bore a certain semblance and likeness to wise men.

For these reasons it is unlawful either to weigh true morality against conflicting expediency, or common morality, which is cultivated by those who wish to be considered good men, against what is profitable; but we every-day people must observe and live up to that moral right which comes within the range of our comprehension 's jealously as the truly wise men have to observe and live to that which is morally right in the technical and true of the word. For otherwise we cannot maintain such s as we have made in the direction of virtue.

So much for those who have won a reputation for being good men by their careful observance of duty.